"Jane Kirby does a great job critically engaging historical and contemporary concerns of the reproductive rights movement in this primer, and shows that the next generation is interested in pushing the conversation forward in an intersectional way."

— KAREN STOTE, author of *An Act of Genocide: Colonialism and the Sterilization of Aboriginal Women in Canada*

"A fascinating exploration of the myths and facts surrounding reproductive justice and abortion. Something every activist needs to have in their back pocket."

— COLLEEN MACQUARRIE, professor of psychology, University of Prince Edward Island, and academic activist

"Kirby helps to move us beyond the privileged concept of being 'pro-choice' by framing access to contraception and abortion as human rights issues that are deeply connected to poverty, racism, cis-sexism, and heterosexism."

— JESSICA SHAW, professor of social work and abortion researcher

"Kirby's book explains in simple language the connection between reproduction and larger systems of oppression. It is an important contribution to literature on reproductive rights."

— BOMA BROWN, founder, Support Network for Indigenous Women & Women of Colour (SNIWWOC)

"Kirby provides an engaging and inspiring account of the reproductive rights movement. Her book pays tribute to women of colour activism and acknowledges the challenges and contradictions of feminist organizing. It will be useful for educators and activists, helping to build feminist solidarity beyond the concept of individual rights and toward notions of justice and responsibility."

— RUTHANN LEE, community organizer and professor

"Kirby's thorough and accessible guide contextualizes today's reproductive issues in historical efforts to secure reproductive rights and reproductive justice. Shedding light on the social justice movements that continue to shape this struggle, *Fired Up about Reproductive Rights* provides a clear and insightful introduction to a multifaceted and pressing issue."

— CYNTHIA SPRING, co-founder of *GUTS magazine*

"*Fired Up about Reproductive Rights* brilliantly untangles complexity and presents a clear and accessible primer on reproductive politics. This book is a must-read for young people."

— ARDATH WHYNACHT, youth advocate and professor of sociology

FIRED UP ABOUT
REPRODUCTIVE RIGHTS

JANE KIRBY

Between the Lines
Toronto

First published in 2017 by Between the Lines
401 Richmond Street West
Studio 277
Toronto, Ontario M5V 3A8
Canada
1-800-718-7201
www.btlbooks.com

Library and Archives Canada Cataloguing in Publication

Kirby, Jane, 1986–, author
Fired up about reproductive rights / Jane Kirby.
(Fired up)

Includes index.
Issued in print and electronic formats.

ISBN 978-1-77113-209-1 (softcover).—ISBN 978-1-77113-210-7 (EPUB).—
ISBN 978-1-77113-211-4 (PDF)

1. Reproductive rights.   2. Sexual rights.   3. Birth control—Social aspects.
4. Contraception—Social aspects.   5. Women's rights.   6. Feminism.   I. Title.

HQ766.K57 2017   305.42   C2016-907420-X
C2016-907421-8

Cover design by Jennifer Tiberio
Cover illustration by Jack Dylan
Text design by Gordon Robertson
Printed in Canada

We acknowledge for their financial support of our publishing activities the Government of Canada through the Canada Book Fund, the Canada Council for the Arts, which last year invested $153 million to bring the arts to Canadians throughout the country, and the Government of Ontario through the Ontario Arts Council, the Ontario Book Publishers Tax Credit program, and the Ontario Media Development Corporation.

CONTENTS

ACKNOWLEDGEMENTS

Writing even this short book was an enormous undertaking that would not have been possible without the generosity and support of a good number of people:

The entire team at Between the Lines. Particularly my editor Amanda for her insight, patience, and guidance through the process, and Tilman for his invaluable copyediting that contributed to a much clearer and more accessible manuscript.

My anonymous readers, whose feedback was vital in improving and shaping the final drafts of the book. A particular thank you to Jessica Shaw, whose feedback and conversation helped me overcome some difficult tensions I was facing in the writing process.

Melissa Marie (emmy) Legge, Elaine, Doulton, April, and Jenna for their encouragement and feedback on earlier drafts of the book. Melissa B. and Doulton for agreeing to share their thoughts in an interview.

My partner, David, for supporting me throughout the writing process and cooking me dinner on late nights. To my family for their unwavering support (sometimes even in the face of political differences), and especially to my mom, for being a supporter of all my writing projects, my faithful proofreader, and my first feminist influence.

All those working in the fight for social justice, particularly those I have been privileged enough to work alongside, for sharing your courage, knowledge, and belief that we can do better.

INTRODUCTION

I GREW UP in a Catholic family in the suburbs of Toronto, where I went to a religious high school and attended church regularly. So my access to education on sexual and reproductive health was rather limited. I vividly remember one male high school religion teacher. He told us that girls and women who had abortions were not only selfish, they were immoral. I also remember what my gym teacher told us. She was forced to say one thing as part of the Catholic high school curriculum, but she said that if we ever found ourselves in "trouble," she would give us different advice as our friend. It was no secret that trouble, for a Catholic teenage girl, meant pregnant.

This created a rather difficult situation for anyone who got pregnant. Have an abortion and be forced to live with guilt. Or keep the child and be seen forever as someone who got herself in trouble. No one gave us information about condoms or the pill. The point was to keep us from having sex at all. The boys, for some reason, were given no such instruction.

To her credit, my gym teacher made an important acknowledgement. Sometimes the rules of the establishment don't really fit with the reality of our lives. Of course many of us did have sex as teens. And, in an environment where birth control was a taboo, some got pregnant. The school system was not too supportive of young single mothers. Those who went through with their pregnancies almost always dropped out of school. Their conspicuous absence would be discussed in hushed tones behind locker doors. But at my high school, at least, abortion was not something you talked about. Beyond rumours, you never really knew who might have had one.

Despite feeling a good deal of confusion, born of guilt, I could see the consequences that pregnancy had on my peers. That convinced me early on that for some people abortion was a necessary choice—if not one to be taken lightly. My gym teacher must have agreed. She recognized that things were not always clear-cut. It is difficult to go to school while raising a newborn. Few schools have a daycare, allow for breastfeeding, or offer flexible schedules. So many people might choose to have an abortion in order to continue with their education. There are many different reasons someone might choose to have an abortion. They can't afford to raise a child. They want to pursue a career. They don't want a relationship with the man who got them pregnant. For health reasons or for fears for the health of the child. To better take care of children they already have. There are as many good reasons for a woman to have an abortion as there are women. In any of these circumstances, the inability to access an abortion might have long-term negative consequences on their lives.

In my experience, many Catholics question the church's disdain for allowing women to control whether they have children. It seems to have more to do with male authority than with anything else. My religion teacher presented the abortion debate as a moral question of when life begins. But many women and trans people know from experience that the struggle for abortion rights is part of a broader struggle to allow us to control our own bodies.

As American civil rights campaigner Flo Kennedy once said, "If men could get pregnant, abortion would be a sacrament." Women are discouraged from accessing abortions, but they aren't supported in becoming mothers. They are put in these no-win situations because dominant cultures and religions are patriarchal—or more specifically, heteropatriarchal. The term "patriarchy" describes the way that our cultures, religions, and economic systems were crafted by men to serve the interests of men. "Heteropatriarchy" takes this concept a step further: the dominant culture assumes heterosexuality as the norm and enforces a strict gender divide between men and women. Heteropatriarchy influences how our relationships and families are structured. It also plays a key role in maintaining nation-states and the capitalist economic system. Reproduction is usually seen as the domain of women and a marker of heterosexual relationships. So control of reproduction is important to the continued survival of the patriarchal system.

Though we tend to take the patriarchy for granted, it relies on several myths that are perpetuated by those in power. Many of these myths have to do with reproduction.

MYTH 1
REPRODUCTIVE ISSUES ARE ISSUES OF MORALITY

In the media, reproductive issues are often treated as moral questions. That is, they are discussed in the context of a value system that may be associated with religious doctrine. Debates about abortion, teen pregnancy, and sex ed are presented as a difference of opinion about what is right or wrong.

But what forces shape how we decide what is right and wrong? In many parts of the world, economically privileged men occupy both formal and informal positions of power. They can influence society's moral compass to their own benefit. Even where men aren't in power, our social and economic structures are built on standards of morality that favour men.

This is why when an unmarried teenager gets pregnant, she may be treated as immoral. She may be forced to continue with an unwanted pregnancy but denied adequate social supports to raise a child. And this is seen as a just punishment. The man who got her pregnant faces few consequences. A patriarchal system helps men maintain their power both at the political level and in intimate relationships. Seeing reproductive issues as moral issues is itself a political choice. It is a choice that distracts from the power relations at the heart of the question.

The feminist movement in the 1960s and 1970s demanded access to contraceptives and abortion. Many in the anti-abortion movement argue that this was a threat to morality. Feminists counter that they were allowing women to express their sexuality more freely, in ways that have always been enjoyed by men. Feminists challenged the status quo, which tried to limit women's control over their own bodies and lives. *The personal is political*, they said. Decisions that seem to be individual, that is, are often shaped by larger political agendas.

Reproductive issues are political for other reasons too. Reproduction is central to the organization of the economy. Children must be raised to be workers. Birthing and raising children is usually unpaid work, but this reproductive labour is essential. Governments and corporations encourage people at times to have children and discourage them at others. One poignant example is a U.S. government–funded campaign to encourage the sterilization of Puerto Rican women in the 1930s to 1960s.[1] American sugar companies in the territory needed more workers for their operations, and preventing women from having children was a way to get them out of the house and into the workforce.

The sterilization campaign in Puerto Rico was also an expression of racism—and in this respect it is far from an anomaly. In addition to patriarchy, the interrelated systems of colonialism, white supremacy, and settler colonialism motivate state control over reproduction.

Dictating who can have children, how many, and under what circumstances is a tool of state power. To protect political and economic interests, governments often encourage some people to have children and prevent others from doing so. For example, before slavery was abolished in the United States, slave owners valued the

Colonialism, White Supremacy, and Settler Colonialism

"Colonialism" refers to a state dominating another region to secure land, labour, and resources. In the fifteenth century, Europeans began to explore and dominate the rest of the world. Most places that were colonized have seen vibrant resistance movements. Colonial power relations still exist, though.

"White supremacy" is the belief that white people are superior to people of colour, and the systems that reinforce this power. White supremacy made it seem acceptable to conquer inhabited territories. It also justified the dehumanization of black people necessary for slavery. And its legacy continues today in the ongoing power relationship of white people over people of colour.

"Settler colonialism" describes the ongoing colonialism in places like Canada, the United States, New Zealand, and Australia. Here, settlers established nation-states where a white population continues to dominate Indigenous people. European explorers could not claim to have "discovered" these countries if they acknowledged the civilizations already living there. In order to establish colonies, and eventually nation-states, settlers needed to eliminate or assimilate the Indigenous population.

Indigenous people have been targeted for sterilization and had their children taken and put into residential schools or foster care. This is not a product of simple discrimination. It is part of a bigger project to destroy Indigenous communities, directly by reducing their population or indirectly by destroying their cultures and identity.

ability of black women to give birth. Black women's children would be born into slavery. So their reproductive lives were controlled to maintain the slave labour force.[2] Since abolition, there have been efforts to limit the black population. Now, the motivation is to avoid any challenge to the white-dominated social order.

Canada, the United States, New Zealand, and Australia were established on inhabited territories. One way these states have sought to reduce and dominate Indigenous populations is by controlling their reproduction. That is, by preventing them from having children or from raising the children they have.[3]

There is also a history of compulsory sterilization practices. In the United States, involuntary sterilization campaigns have targeted black, Indigenous, and immigrant women. Many women were sterilized without their consent (or their knowledge) while in hospital for other procedures. Countries including Germany, Sweden, Switzerland, Japan, and Russia have initiated campaigns to "improve" the breeding stock and sterilize disabled people. In Canada, two provinces had compulsory sterilization laws until the 1970s. Those targeted for sterilization came mostly from low-income backgrounds and were disproportionately Indigenous.

In the Global South, a rhetoric of population control has accompanied many development projects. It has been influenced by the power differential that still exists between the Global North and countries that had been colonized. During the 1960s, for example, Canadian volunteers with CUSO—a non-governmental organization similar to the U.S. Peace Corps—worked in family planning clinics that distributed birth control in India.[4] This initiative was part of significant foreign involvement in "modernizing" India. Birth control, though, was not legal in Canada until 1969. It was seen as a more appropriate solution in India than in Canada. And it was promoted to reduce the population of poor women, not to give women choices.

This shameful recent history is the other side to the struggle for reproductive rights. While middle-class white women campaign to access abortions, many women of colour, Indigenous people, trans people, and disabled people are prevented from having children at all. Racism, colonialism, and discrimination against disabled people motivate state control of people's bodies.

When we look at struggles over reproductive issues in this way, we can see that issues of power and control, not morality, are at their core. Control over reproduction has been used as a tool of oppression and domination. Reproductive issues are, in fact, issues of social justice.[5]

MYTH 2
REPRODUCTIVE ISSUES ARE YOUR GRANDMOTHER'S ISSUE

I used to think that the battle for reproductive control was a concern of my mother's generation. When I was a teen, I didn't feel feminism was relevant anymore. Maybe it had been once. But for me, it was pretty much confined to history class—and rarely talked about there. The fight for reproductive rights conjured images of women burning their bras in the 1960s and 1970s—the period known as second-wave feminism. It was hard to figure out what that had to do with the problems my friends and I were facing.

Now, it's true that many battles for control of our own bodies were fought and won by previous generations. We can thank these activists for the sexual and reproductive rights that many of us enjoy, including expanded legal access to sex ed, contraception, and abortion. But the gains of previous generations were also limited. And there is an ongoing fight to prevent existing rights from being stripped away. If abortion is legal where you live, you might think that abortion access is no longer an issue. Where I live, in Canada, the law that made abortion illegal except to protect the health of the mother was struck down in 1988. So I thought things were fine here, until I moved to the east coast to go to university.

In Halifax, Nova Scotia, a major urban centre and home to the province's primary hospital that provided abortions, several of my

Waves of Feminism

The "waves" of the feminist movement refer to its historical phases in Europe and North America. The phases are characterized by what issues are at the forefront and who is driving the conversation.

First wave: Usually dated to the late nineteenth and early twentieth centuries, the focus was on opening opportunities for women, especially in the political sphere. The major achievement was the right to vote, though this right was often limited to wealthy white women.

Second wave: Amid the upheaval of the U.S. civil rights and anti–Vietnam War movements, feminist concerns began broadening in the 1960s to include sexuality, reproduction, and other issues in the family and workplace. Domestic violence came to the forefront, and rape crisis centres were established. Women won victories for contraception and other reproductive rights, more workplace equity, and the establishment of women's only spaces. The distinction between biological sex and socially constructed gender was also drawn. Given the frequent overlap between feminist, anti-war, and civil rights organizing, women of colour were involved.

Third wave: Sometimes known as post-colonial feminism, this wave began in the early 1990s. It is driven by the voices of women of colour, women from the Global South, and queer women. The third wave emerged out of a critique of the way second-wave feminism, while including women of colour, was dominated by the perspectives of white women. This diverse movement advocates for an intersectional perspective, which sees gender, race, class, and sexuality as mutually reinforcing and overlapping sets of experiences and oppressions. Women are also fiercely exerting their right to cultural self-expression.

friends struggled to access abortion services. When they called the hospital, they encountered staff who didn't know where to direct them. Some faced long wait times. And getting an abortion was even more difficult, I learned, in the rest of the province. In fact, across the country, a 2006 study showed that only 16 percent of hospitals provide abortion services.[6] People in rural areas and the north face particular barriers, as the cost of travelling for an abortion can be out of reach.

A similar situation exists in the United States. Although abortion was legalized in 1973, abortion services can be hard to come by. The states of Mississippi, North Dakota, South Dakota, and Wyoming each have only one abortion clinic. In recent years, clinics across the country have been closing fast. Lack of universal health care and limits to the use of federal funds to pay for abortions only compound this problem. In Turkey, abortion has since 1983 been legal in all circumstances during the first trimester of pregnancy. But only 3 out of 37 hospitals provide the procedure. In Austria, abortion is theoretically available on demand, but outside of major cities like Vienna it can be difficult to obtain. Costs at clinics outside of public hospitals are often so high that it can be cheaper to travel to another country to get an abortion.[7]

Feminists of the past achieved some legal wins around these issues. In many parts of the world today, abortion is a simple, safe, and legal medical procedure. But as you can see, the wins of the past haven't gone far enough. In many places where abortion is legal, accessing it isn't all that simple. Often doctors don't know, or aren't willing to tell you, where to go for an abortion. It's up to you to research your options. If you don't live in a major city, you'll likely have to travel several hours to get the procedure. This might mean taking time off school or work, finding childcare, and paying for transportation and a hotel. It can get expensive quickly. You'll also have to find out if your health insurance covers the procedure or not. In many places, abortions aren't covered by publicly funded insurance, so you'll also have to cover the cost yourself. If you're lucky, you have parents or friends from whom you can borrow the money without fielding too many questions. There's still a fair bit of stigma, so you may well prefer to keep your pregnancy a secret.

If you're in an underserviced area, you likely won't be able to book an appointment right away, so you'll have to endure the effects of pregnancy while you wait. And depending on local laws and policies, it might take several trips to the clinic. In some places you'll have to get a parental consent form signed. So much for keeping your pregnancy a secret. You may have to watch mandatory (but medically unnecessary) ultrasounds, or face a required waiting period. Hopefully you caught your pregnancy early, since most places will only provide abortions early in the pregnancy.

These are just the logistical hoops. In many places, you'll also face anti-abortion protesters outside of clinics. Hospital staff may be paternalistic and condescending. And you may face the misunderstanding and judgment of people you thought were friends.

Try reading the paragraphs above replacing "abortion" with "getting your tonsils removed" and "pregnancy" with "tonsillitis." Applied to most safe, straightforward medical procedures, this scenario quickly starts to sound ridiculous.

The situation is more difficult in countries that still have prohibitive abortion laws. In Ireland and Northern Ireland, abortion is allowed only to save a woman's life. In Poland, it is allowed only under the most severe threats to a woman's physical health or in cases of rape or incest. Countries like Chile, Nicaragua, El Salvador, and Malta have total abortion bans—abortions are not permitted even to save a woman's life. Women in El Salvador have been jailed after swearing they naturally miscarried. Even if the fetus is known to be unviable—with a serious heart defect that means it could never be born alive, for example—women in these countries are forced to carry their pregnancy to term. They must endure serious physical changes and a chorus of congratulations for a child that will never live.[8]

When someone feels that they cannot or do not want to have a child, a lack of legal access to safe, professional abortion services is often not enough to stop them. The evidence on that is clear. In

Chile, the wealthy fly to the United States or another country with more liberal laws. People who can't afford that seek out underground illegal abortions, despite a litany of health risks and the threat of up to five years' jail time. Each year, an estimated 20 million women worldwide have unsafe abortions.[9] The vast majority of these abortions take place in the Global South. But do-it-yourself abortions—often in unsafe conditions and without professional oversight—are common anywhere that access to safer services is limited. That's why the coat hanger—which, despite very real safety risks, has sometimes been used as a method to remove the fetus and induce an abortion—has become a symbol in the struggle for abortion access. In the most extreme cases, the lack of access to safe abortion services can be fatal. The World Health Organization estimates that 47,000 women die each year as a result of complications from unsafe abortions.

Statistics like these make me furious. The struggle for abortion access is a struggle for people's lives. This was true in the past, and it remains true now. And you face the most barriers to access and the biggest risks if you don't have the money to jump through the hoops to access safe services. The battle for safe, legal, and accessible abortion services is not your grandmother's issue. It's not over yet, even in places where it began long ago.

MYTH 3
ABORTION IS THE ONLY REPRODUCTIVE ISSUE

Reproductive justice is more than the right to not have children. It includes the right to have children, control birthing options, parent your children, and raise them in safe, healthy communities. It is also about fighting the systems that encourage state control over people's bodies—like patriarchy, racism, colonialism, and capitalism.[10] Today's struggles for reproductive justice include many issues that got little attention from the historical feminist movement. The struggle against coercive sterilization, for example. The voices of disabled people, queer and trans folks, Indigenous people, people of colour, and people from lower-income backgrounds were under-represented in mainstream feminism. These voices have expanded reproductive activism beyond contraception and abortion. Activists now also critique campaigns to limit the reproduction of those deemed "undesirable" by the state or society. They point out the many barriers that people who want to have families face. They suggest that reproduction cannot be separated from other struggles for justice. In writing this book, as a middle-class white woman, I have been inspired by many activists, friends, writers, and advocates whose experiences differ dramatically from my own.

For example, consider who gets to parent and who is considered a good or bad parent. If a teen decides that having a child is the best option for them, they will often be stigmatized and seen as unfit. This is doubly true for young people of colour or from lower-income backgrounds. Reproductive justice means supporting the decisions of all teens. It means promoting support systems to help young families. Sadly, child welfare authorities are more likely to take children away from parents who are struggling—even just to pay the rent—than to offered substantive support.

Families who do not fit the traditional nuclear family structure also have to fight for their right to have children. Single mothers face stigma, for example. Many people think a child needs a father figure. Men are supposed to be strong and stoic providers, they believe, and women more emotional and caring. Thus, a "natural" balance is achieved with opposite-sex attraction and reproduction. But these are just stereotypes. Activism in the feminist and the LGBTQ (lesbian, gay, bisexual, transgender, and queer) communities has gone a long way in challenging them. Still the idea persists that the only families fit to reproduce and to raise children are those with two parents—one male, one female.

For same-sex couples and the broader LGBTQ community, parenting children—through adoption, surrogacy, or co-parenting—challenges this cultural norm. So their options may be limited. Trans people, or people who don't readily identify with one gender, have an even bigger challenge to access parenthood. When trans men wish to get pregnant, they face particularly high levels of misunderstanding from medical professionals and the general public.

The distinction between fit or unfit parents is also linked to bigger political issues. The United States has a long history of anti-black racism. As a result, black children are more likely to be taken from their families and put in foster care. In 2012, African American children represented 26 percent of children in care, despite accounting for only 14 percent of the child population.[11]

Parenting is a means of transmitting culture. So determining who is allowed to raise a child can be a strategy for eliminating unwanted cultures. In other words, for carrying out genocide. And settler states as we know them exist because of genocidal relationships with Indigenous peoples.

In Australia, it was government policy until 1969 to remove Aboriginal children from their families. The intention was to destroy Aboriginal culture, language, and spirituality. Some children who had been placed in institutions or with foster parents never saw their families again. Children of mixed Aboriginal and white descent were particularly targeted. They were thought to be easier candidates for assimilation. Known as the Stolen Generation, many of these children suffered abuse while in care. Many still suffer from mental health concerns as a result.[12]

Likewise, Canada has an abominable history of residential schooling. Indigenous children were taken from their families and forced into boarding schools. They were denied access to their languages and cultures. Many faced physical and sexual abuse. The refusal to let Indigenous families parent their own children was an attempt, as an Indian Affairs agent famously stated, "to kill the Indian in the child." Indigenous children were also placed in foster care at a disproportionate rate in the 1960s through the 1980s. The rate at which Indigenous children were removed from their families and placed in state care accelerated during this time period to such an extent that the phenomenon was known as the Sixties Scoop.

Anti-Black Racism and Reproduction

White supremacy determines not only who is considered an ideal citizen but also who is allowed or encouraged to reproduce. Racist stereotypes treat people of colour as sexually irresponsible and incapable of proper parenting. Particularly in the United States, black people have been cast as sexualized Jezebels, devious welfare recipients, and negligent mothers. These stereotypes justify campaigns denying black parenthood.*

Historically, a motivation of the campaign for birth control was to limit the black birth rate. The American Birth Control League, along with Planned Parenthood founder Margaret Sanger, campaigned for birth control in part to contain the black population. Of the 7,686 sterilizations carried out as part of a eugenics campaign by North Carolina in the 1930s to the 1960s, approximately 5,000 were targeted at black women.† More recently, dangerous long-acting contraceptives have been pushed on black communities—the first pilot program for Norplant in a high school occurred at a Baltimore school where all but 5 of 350 students were black.‡

Black people continue to face high rates of poverty, incarceration, and violence (including state violence). This prevents them from making free decisions about their reproduction. It should come as no surprise that it was black women who coined the term "reproductive justice" and that black-led organizations spearhead the reproductive justice movement.

* Dorothy Roberts, *Killing the Black Body: Race, Reproduction and the Meaning of Liberty* (New York: Random House, 1997), 10–19.

† Angela Davis, *Women, Race and Class* (New York: Random House, 1982), 360–2.

‡ Roberts, 114.

Boarding schools for Indigenous children also existed in the United States. They had similar goals of destroying Native American culture to make way for the country's westward expansion.

Entire generations were prevented from parenting their own children. Because children's experiences in residential schools were so traumatic, many social problems that plague Indigenous communities have been blamed on the legacy of these schools. Survivors lacked the benefit of being parented themselves and experienced abuse in the schools. Many have passed this legacy on to their children, continuing a cycle of abuse and intergenerational trauma.

In all three countries this colonial legacy continues. Native American youth are put into foster care at 1.6 times the expected rate. In Australia, nearly 15,000 Aboriginal children were in out-of-home care in 2014. And in Canada today, it is estimated that there are three times as many Indigenous children in the foster care system as there were in the residential school system at its height.[13]

When Indigenous people are targeted for sterilization campaigns or have their children taken away, it is more than simple discrimination. These actions are part of the colonial project. Indigenous populations are also eliminated through assimilation, including by criteria about who qualifies as Indigenous. In the United States, tribal membership is often related to "blood quantum." In Canada, indigeneity is defined by the Indian Act. The definition discriminates against women and ensures a decline in the population of status Indians. Mi'kmaw lawyer Pamela Palmater has said this policy can only be understood in line with Canadian policy to find "the final solution of the Indian Problem."[14]

These are some of the ways that settler colonialism has driven reproduction and population control. Jessica Danforth, executive director of the Native Youth Sexual Health Network, argues that reproductive justice has a long history in Indigenous communities. Prior to colonization, Indigenous communities recognized sex ed, abortion rights, and gender fluidity. In listening to wisdom gained from this ancestral history and the continued resistance of

Indigenous people and people of colour, there is much to learn. Fighting colonial policy is not tangential to reproductive concerns. It is part of a holistic vision for justice.

Reproductive oppression, as these examples show, is deeply entwined with other systems of oppression. This short book focuses primarily on abortion and coercive sterilization. But that's really only scratching the surface. The fight against workplace toxins that cause miscarriage and birth defects is a reproductive issue. So are the struggle for access to universal childcare and many other struggles.

MYTH 4

THESE ARE ONLY WOMEN'S ISSUES

When we broaden our ideas of what reproductive issues are, it's clear that they don't just matter to women. For example, we touched on the history of boarding schools for Indigenous people. If you care about fighting colonialism, racism, and genocide, think about the right to parent children. Forced and coerced sterilization has taken place around the world. If you care about fighting discrimination based on race, ethnicity, and ability, consider the right to have children.

Men are also affected by the restriction of women's reproductive rights. If a woman has an unwanted pregnancy and is forced to carry it to term, male partners are affected. Men don't face the same physical and emotional repercussions as women, and they aren't stigmatized in the same way. But unwanted pregnancies still affect them. And as Nasim Pedrad quipped on *Saturday Night Live*, "If men could get pregnant, abortion clinics would be like Starbucks: two on every corner and four in every airport." Likewise, women are most often the target of coercive sterilization campaigns. But men have also been targeted in many countries.

Historically men have made up a significant proportion of the anti-abortion movement. Men are also more likely to occupy positions of power in society, so it is important to have male allies. These

Gender and Reproductive Justice

Heteropatriarchy has entrenched the power of men over women. It also helped entrench "man" and "woman" as discrete categories, and the assumption that our lived gender experience lines up neatly with the sex we are assigned at birth. Activism in the queer and trans community is challenging these ideas by recognizing the fluidity of gender.

"Cisgender" refers to anyone who lives and identifies with the gender they were assigned at birth. For example, cis women are women who were designated female at birth and continue to identify as women. Cis men are men who were designated male at birth and identify as men. In contrast, "transgender" refers to anyone who lives and identifies as a gender other than what they were assigned at birth. Trans men are men who were designated female at birth but identify as men; trans women are women who were designated male at birth and identify as women. "Gender queer" people fall elsewhere on the spectrum between male and female, or reject the notion of two genders entirely.

Gender fluidity complicates our understanding of reproduction. Much of the existing research refers to the experience of cisgender women. We are only beginning to recognize that people with other gender identities can get pregnant. When I use the gendered term "women" in this book, I'm usually referring to research that deals specifically with cisgender women. But much of what I'm discussing might also apply to trans women, trans men, or gender queer people. In fact, because non-binary identities can be poorly understood by the medical community, they often face additional barriers to accessing reproductive health care and support.

struggles should rightly be led by women and queer and trans folks, who face more policing of their bodies and limits to their reproductive choices. But men also have an important role to play.

Furthermore, gender is more complex than a simple division between men and women. For example, it is possible for trans men to get pregnant and for trans women to get their partners pregnant. Access to contraception and abortion can be particularly important in these cases. Pregnancy may not fit with a queer or trans person's sexual and gender identity. But hormonal contraceptives like the birth control pill have not been tested for use on trans people.[15] On the flip side, queer and trans people may want to have children. When they do, they may face prohibitively expensive procedures and a good deal of misunderstanding from the medical community and society at large. In some countries, trans people must be sterilized to have a change of gender legally recognized. They are denied the ability to make decisions about their bodies and reproductive capacities.

WHAT'S IT GOT TO DO WITH ME?

Have you heard the saying, I'll bet you one unplanned pregnancy that you're secretly pro-choice? Where I live, in Canada, almost a third of women will have an abortion. This is in a country with relatively easy access to contraception. The morning-after pill, which retroactively prevents a pregnancy, is available over the counter. Information on safer sex is easy to come by. In places where measures to reduce unwanted pregnancy are less available, the rate of women needing abortions is likely to be even higher.

Using contraception decreases the likelihood of needing an abortion. But no matter how careful you are, no method of contraception is 100 percent effective. If you are a woman who is sexually active with men, the odds are pretty high that at some point in your life you might need an abortion. If you are a man, a partner might need one. Even if you never decide to get an abortion, a friend, family member, or colleague of yours probably will. And consider the possibility that you or someone you care about might be sterilized without their consent or be otherwise denied the ability to have or parent wanted children.

Each of our lives is affected by issues of reproduction. These concerns are not just intimate or individual problems. Every time someone gets pregnant and has to navigate policies, stereotypes, economic conditions, and other barriers that prevent them from making an entirely free decision, bigger political agendas are at play. Which brings in the fight against economic inequality, sexism, racism, homophobia, and restricted access to health care and education. You may currently be facing choices related to pregnancy or your reproductive health. Or you may not be directly affected by reproductive issues at this time. But if you care about social justice, it is important to pay attention to issues of reproduction.

1

DEFINING REPRODUCTIVE ISSUES

WHEN I FIRST started learning about reproductive issues, I encountered some pretty confusing terminology. Reproductive rights, reproductive health, reproductive justice. Reproductive freedom, pro-choice . . . what next? The communities that work on these issues are diverse, and people choose the words they use for different reasons. Some of these terms can be used interchangeably. But I learned that they can also have distinct meanings and represent different political positions.

Words carry power, and the language that activists use can shape which issues they see as most important. The distinctions between reproductive rights, health, and justice grew out of the work of movements and organizations—particularly the efforts of women of colour in the United States.[1] We've already encountered some of these terms in the introduction. Let's take a closer look at them.

REPRODUCTIVE RIGHTS

"Reproductive rights" may be the most familiar term. By reproductive rights, we usually mean the legal right to contraception or abortion. When access to abortion became legal in the United Kingdom (except Northern Ireland) in 1967, the United States in 1973, and Italy in 1978, people gained a reproductive right.

We often use "rights" for what we think people should be entitled to in society. Food, water, health, security, and freedom from discrimination are rights. If you support reproductive rights, it means that you believe people should be entitled to access services like contraception and abortion. A 2015 United Nations report affirmed that reproductive rights are human rights. It stated, "We must ensure women, youth and children have access to the full range of health services," including reproductive rights.[2]

Anything that stands in the way of access—cost, geography, restrictive laws—might be seen as a threat to reproductive rights. Technically, though, rights refers to guaranteeing these things legally—through laws, policies, charters, and court decisions. It is less about other ways of making sure people can use these services. That is, a rights model is primarily concerned with whether someone is breaking the law when they buy birth control or get an abortion, and whether a doctor is breaking the law by providing these options. It doesn't consider whether birth control and abortion providers are conveniently available in every community.

A reproductive right is usually framed in positive terms—as something gained through a legal decision. But in many cases, getting rid of laws that prevent people from accessing their rights is even more important. In Canada, for example, feminists fought to strike down the law prohibiting abortion. Once the law was removed in the late 1980s, people were able to access the procedure more safely and easily. (In this case, abortion was decriminalized. It wasn't legally guaranteed, but it was no longer a criminal act.) Likewise, sterilization laws in two Canadian provinces were scrapped in the early 1970s. This meant that people would no longer be subject to state-sponsored sterilization campaigns. They gained the right to have children.

With its focus on the right to be free from state intervention, a rights approach is related to the term "reproductive freedom." The

fight for reproductive rights is therefore often framed as protecting the "right to choose" and "right to privacy."

Rights organizations usually address their arguments to politicians and the courts. They might lobby government represen-
tatives, encourage people to vote for pro-choice candidates, or
challenge laws in the courts. In some countries legal reproductive
rights are still very limited. In these countries, rights activists focus
on eliminating laws that prohibit birth control and abortion, or
passing laws that make them legal.

For example, the Abortion Rights Campaign in Ireland advocates for the removal of the Eighth Amendment, which crimi-
nalizes abortion unless continuing the pregnancy would result
in death. Under the current laws, it is unclear to physicians under
what circumstances they can provide abortions. So activists also
advocate for legislation that clarifies for whom, when, where, and
how abortions can be legally performed. They maintain an active
social media presence, hold an annual March for Choice, and provide safe spaces for women to tell their stories.

Where abortion and other reproductive services are legal, rights
organizations focus on preventing new laws that would threaten
this status and abolishing laws that inhibit access. For example,
in the United Kingdom, the Abortion Rights organization fights
against legal attacks on reproductive freedom—like measures to
reduce the time period during which abortions are allowed. It also
works to improve the current abortion law. Abortions are practically available in the United Kingdom up to twenty-four weeks. But
two doctors must assert that having an abortion is less a threat to
the person's physical and mental health than continuing with the
pregnancy. In other words, abortion is not available "on demand" in
the United Kingdom. This is because the Abortion Act 1967 did not
actually decriminalize abortion. It just permitted it under certain
circumstances. Abortion Rights is working to change this situation.

It is necessary and important to fight for reproductive rights. If
people have to break laws to access abortion services, the services
are less accessible and less safe. But focusing only on rights has its

Some Reproductive Rights Milestones

1966 Mississippi becomes first U.S. state to legalize abortion in cases of rape.

1967 The Abortion Act legalizes abortions in some circumstances in the United Kingdom (except Northern Ireland).

1969 Canada decriminalizes contraception and begins to loosen restrictions on abortion laws, allowing abortions with the approval of Therapeutic Abortion Committees.

1973 The U.S. Supreme Court's *Roe v. Wade* decision declares bans on abortions unconstitutional before fetal viability (i.e., in the first trimester); states may choose to impose restrictions thereafter, unless continuing with the pregnancy poses a threat to the woman's health.

1983 In Ireland, the constitution is changed to give rights to the unborn, a move designed to prevent the legalization of abortion.

1988 The abortion pill is made legal in France.

1988 The Morgentaler decision of the Supreme Court effectively decriminalizes abortion in Canada.

1993 Poland bans abortion in most circumstances.

2007 Mexico City decriminalizes abortion in first twelve weeks of pregnancy.

2015 A UN report affirms that women's rights—including reproductive rights—are human rights.

limitations. By stressing the legality of abortion, rights activists may ignore other factors—like geography and income—that affect access to abortion services, as well as an array of other reproductive issues.

Sometimes even policies that directly influence access to abortion are not taken seriously by reproductive rights organizations.

One example is the response to the Hyde Amendment. This U.S. policy prohibits the use of federal funds for abortions in most circumstances. The policy was introduced in 1976 as a response to the Supreme Court's *Roe v. Wade* decision, which effectively legalized abortion on the grounds of the right to privacy. The amendment meant that Medicaid, the federal health insurance program, would no longer cover abortions. This seriously limited low-income people's ability to access the procedure. However, there was little opposition from most mainstream reproductive rights organizations. Members felt that the legal status of abortion was enough, overlooking the many other factors that can prevent someone from accessing an abortion.

REPRODUCTIVE HEALTH

A reproductive health approach focuses on people's immediate reproductive and sexual health needs. Organizations that use this approach develop awareness campaigns and educational resources. They train doctors to provide abortions and educate people about safer sex. They offer birth control, information about menopause and menstruation, and counselling about pregnancy options. They test for pregnancy or sexually transmitted infections, and provide abortion services or referrals. Obstetricians and midwives work in the field of reproductive health. Planned Parenthood is one internationally known organization that provides sexual and reproductive health care and education.

In many places, reproductive health organizations have offered their services even when those services were illegal. Henry Morgentaler is one example. After testifying before a Canadian House of Commons committee in 1967 that women should have the right to a safe abortion, Dr. Morgentaler was contacted by many women seeking abortions. He began performing abortions illegally in his private clinic, and went on to set up private abortion clinics across the country. His work in reproductive health settings often got him into trouble with the law, and he had to defend himself in court. That translated into real gains in reproductive rights. At the Supreme Court of Canada, Morgentaler successfully appealed a decision from a lower court. He argued that the abortion law threatened a woman's right to "life, liberty and security of the person." Against a backdrop of feminist activism calling for improved access to abortion, this case resulted in the decriminalization of abortion in Canada in 1988.

A more recent example is Women on Waves, which provides abortion services, education, and contraceptives from onboard a ship. Based out of the Netherlands, the organization does most of its work outside of territorial boundaries. In international waters, no country's reproductive health laws can be enforced. Women on Waves also works with local organizations to help them fight oppressive laws. And it advocates for the abortion pill—which allows people to access safe, medical abortions in their own homes. Women on Waves sailed to Ireland in 2001, Poland in 2003, Portugal in 2004, Spain in 2008, and Morocco in 2012. Even when the ship was unable to bypass local authorities, it attracted attention and highlighted local campaigns. In Morocco, the government prevented Women on Waves from bringing people on the ship for medical abortions. However, using the resulting media attention, the organization launched a hotline. You could call it to learn how to safely induce an abortion using locally available medication. In 2015, Women on Waves made headlines when it flew the world's first abortion drone over the German border to Poland. The German police tried to intervene, but two Polish women successfully received the abortion pill. This organization's creative approach unites the provision of services with the fight to change restrictive laws.

Reproductive health approaches are valuable, especially when they assist people who are unable to afford birth control or travel to abortion clinics. But some barriers can only be overcome by broader change. Disabled people might not be able to get to a clinic. People with limited incomes might not be able to afford the time off work. People of colour and Indigenous people might face discrimination that will discourage them from accessing health care facilities, or be worried about sterilization abuse. Reproductive health organizations are essential in meeting people's immediate reproductive needs. But unless they have a larger goal of social justice in mind, they are limited in what they can achieve.

REPRODUCTIVE JUSTICE

Reproductive justice is the most holistic approach. The SisterSong Women of Color Reproductive Justice Collective defines it as "the complete physical, mental, spiritual, social, environmental and economic well-being of women and girls, based on the full achievement and protection of women's human rights."[3] For SisterSong, this means fighting for "1) the right to have a child; 2) the right to not have a child; and 3) the right to parent the children we have, as well as control our birthing options."

In other words, this perspective puts the struggle for abortion rights and access alongside other social justice issues. The struggle against forced sterilization and unjust child welfare systems is as important as the struggle for abortion access. Activists with a justice point of view look at all of the barriers—social, legal, political, economic—that might prevent someone from making free decisions about having a child and parenting. They may also look at how control over reproduction supports capitalism, racism, colonialism, and patriarchy.

The term "reproductive justice" is traced to the International Conference on Population and Development that took place in Cairo in 1994. At the conference, a gulf became apparent between two points of view. Some women saw birth control and abortion as important as tools of population control—targeting especially women of colour and women in the Global South. Others saw them as a means of women having control over their own bodies. Both groups were concerned with access to birth control and abortion, but it became apparent that their aims were very much at odds with each other. One side believed strongly in women's rights

What is Intersectionality?

The term "intersectionality" was introduced by black feminist Kimberlé Crenshaw. It means that the experience of multiple oppressions is more than just the sum of its parts. For example, a black woman does not merely experience racism and sexism. She would have a unique experience based on her experience of both. Individuals and communities experience the intersection of many types of oppression around reproductive issues.

Loretta Ross, co-founder of SisterSong, explains that reproductive justice "addresses issues of population control, bodily self-determination, immigrants' rights, economic and environmental justice, sovereignty, and militarism and criminal injustices that limit individual human rights because of group or community oppressions."*

In the United States, mainstream feminist organizations have focused primarily on abortion rights. American women of colour have a long history of organizing for a more complete vision.

* Loretta Ross, "Understanding Reproductive Justice" (SisterSong, 2006, updated 2011), Trust Black Women, www.trustblackwomen.org.

as human rights. The other side believed that human rights could be sacrificed for the goal of population control.

This prompted a Black Women's Caucus at the Illinois Pro-Choice Alliance conference that same year to call for the integration of reproductive health issues with social justice issues. Advocating population control on the backs of vulnerable women, it declared, was not an acceptable stance. Today reproductive justice, a term coined at this meeting, also indicates what is known as an intersectional approach to reproductive issues. In a reproductive justice framework, struggles for gender justice and women's rights are not enough. Reproductive issues must also be understood in terms of the fight against racism, ableism, and class inequality.

Forward Together (formerly Asian Communities for Reproductive Justice), a U.S.-based organization, supports diverse families in a number of ways. It promotes access to health care for LGBTQ communities, advocates for affordable childcare, and supports families who have members in jail. It also produces reports and educational materials. Its 2005 document "A New Vision" first articulated the differences between reproductive rights, health, and justice outlined here. The Native Youth Sexual Health Network works with a reproductive justice framework in Canada and the United States. Its concerns include HIV prevention, fighting trans- and homophobia, combating environmental violence, and advocating for justice for missing and murdered Indigenous women.

Reproductive justice is clearly the most comprehensive approach to reproductive issues. However, systems of oppression won't be dismantled overnight. In the short term, legal protections and service provision remain essential. So ideally, people working in reproductive rights, health, and justice will all work together. For example, reproductive health organizations often strive to make their services accessible in a way that is informed by a reproductive justice approach.

I believe that a justice perspective is the way forward. But this book is titled *Fired Up about Reproductive Rights*. Although I draw on reproductive rights, health, and justice in my own thinking and activism, the next chapters focus on abusive sterilization practices and access to abortion—the right to have and not have children, respectively. It would be impossible to adequately cover all of the issues integral to the justice movement. Issues like racism and colonialism, both central to reproductive justice, deserve their own comprehensive discussion.

Loretta Ross of SisterSong maintains that "reproductive justice is not an exclusive analysis that applies only to women of color."[4] But to avoid replicating the hierarchies that have marked reproductive activism in the past, she is adamant that the movement must be led by the most marginalized. As a white woman from a middle-class background, it therefore seems more appropriate to refer to reproductive rights. More people in my communities will be familiar with this term. My thinking about abortion and coercive sterilization, though, is informed and inspired by the intersectional approach of the reproductive justice movement. I'll be making those connections throughout.

CHOICE VS. CONSENT, ACCESS, AND JUSTICE

Another word that you will hear in conversations about these issues is "choice." Many activists, especially those who work for reproductive rights, use the word a lot. Being "pro-choice" means supporting a person's decision whether or not to have children and supporting legal access to abortion. It is often used in opposition to the anti-abortion movement's framing of its position as "pro-life." But pro-lifers have at times used violent tactics—like attacking abortion providers and bombing clinics—and they often oppose social welfare policies. So many people consider this a misnomer. As comedian George Carlin put it:

> Pro-life conservatives are obsessed with the fetus from conception to nine months. After that, they don't want to know about you. They don't want to hear from you. No nothing. No neonatal care, no daycare, no Head Start, no school lunch, no food stamps, no welfare, no nothing. If you're pre-born, you're fine, if you're preschool, you're fucked.

Instead, because of the anti-abortion movement's disregard for women and trans people's lives and decisions, it may be better labelled "anti-choice."

But the "right to choose" has its own baggage. For one thing, being pro- or anti-choice denotes only your position on abortion. This marginalizes other reproductive concerns. It also isolates the reproductive rights establishment from broader social justice struggles. Reproductive rights organizations may support a politician with pro-choice views. But that same politician may support racist policies or initiatives that will come down hardest on the poor.

Choice is also only meaningful to the extent that it is made free from constraints—financial, social, or otherwise. For people who are wealthy, white, cisgender, and able-bodied, the legal right to abortion may well enable the choice of whether or not to continue with a pregnancy. Well-off white women will generally be supported in having a child. And they will encounter few barriers, beyond some possible stigma, to accessing an abortion. In this case, we might say that the person is able to make a choice about whether or not she prefers to have children.

But for someone who works a minimum wage job and has no health insurance, there may not be much choice in the matter. They can't afford to have an abortion, on the one hand, or raise a child, on the other. Someone might want children, but feel that they are not able to support them. In this case, having an abortion might have more to do with surviving the situation than with what they might otherwise choose. Prominent activist and scholar Angela Davis has pointed to the prevalence of abortion among slave women as exemplary of this situation. Slave women didn't abort their children because they didn't want them. They aborted their children because they couldn't bear the thought of having children born into slavery.[5]

The decisions we make are rarely free from the social, economic, and political contexts that shape our lives. As Loretta Ross has stated, "A woman cannot make an individual decision about her body if she is part of a community whose human rights as a group are violated, such as through environmental dangers or insufficient quality health care."[6]

The state controls reproduction in the context of upholding patriarchy, capitalism, white supremacy, and colonialism. In other words, we can't reduce reproductive issues to a question of individuals being denied options. We also need to consider how power is distributed in our society. While "choice" makes reproductive issues seem personal and individual, collective responses to bigger constraints are called for. For this reason, women of colour have long been vocal in opposing the language of choice. A focus on individual choice ignores the other factors that influence decision-making, as well as the broader implications of individual choices.

Choice is now part of our vocabulary, though. And to be fair, most organizations that use that language have broadened their activities. But it's good to be aware of how the term is used, and when it might obscure some of the bigger issues at play. Personally, I prefer to focus on three pillars that make choice more meaningful: consent, access, and justice.

Consent implies the ability to decide to do something in a way that is informed and entirely voluntary. If you've come across this term before, it was probably in the movement against sexual violence. No always means no when it comes to sex, and anything else is assault. More recently, young feminists have introduced the notion of positive, informed, and enthusiastic consent. Truly consensual sex requires not only the absence of a no, but also the presence of a freely and enthusiastically given yes. A yes that is in any way coerced or not fully informed is not really consent.

Applied to reproductive issues, consent means the opportunity to have full control over what happens to our bodies and to our sexual or reproductive lives. We should be able to have children if we consent to it, or not have children if we don't. Our decisions should be free from any coercion or intervention. And we should have access to all available information.

I like the word "consent" for a few reasons. First, it clarifies the links between the movement against sexual violence and the movement for reproductive rights, health, and justice. Both sexual and reproductive violence are rooted in the inability of people, particularly women and trans people, to have full control over their own bodies. In both cases, having control means having the ability to consent: to sexual encounters and relationships, and to whether, when, and under what circumstances to have children.

Second, consent highlights some issues that have historically been left out of the mainstream feminist movement—particularly the issue of forced sterilization. Lack of consent in this regard has been a central concern in the fight of women of colour, disabled women, trans people, and women in the Global South.

Finally, for me, consent—particularly when combined with access and justice—is a more useful way of thinking about choice. Consent highlights individual decision-making but recognizes that not all decisions are truly consensual. Decisions are only consensual if they are informed, free, and not coerced. This draws attention to the conditions in which we all make choices—conditions that are shaped by social inequality and power relations.

The necessity of access should be clear. If people cannot access what they need to realize their reproductive rights, then they don't really have those rights. My vision of access is far-reaching and inclusive. It includes not just access to services, but also access to information and decision-making power. It means considering who has the access needed to make certain decisions and who does not, and doing what we can to address these gaps.

Access unites the concepts of reproductive rights, health, and justice. If you don't have a car, and no abortion providers, midwives, or sexual health clinics are available by public transit, then your access to these services will be limited. If you are an immigrant and these services are not available in your first language or are not culturally appropriate, your access is limited. If you lack legal immigration status in the country where you are trying to access health care, your access is limited. If contraception and abortion services aren't covered by your health insurance, or if you don't have insurance, your access is limited. If you use a wheelchair but your nearest clinic has no ramp, your access is limited. If you are queer and get pregnant but face doctors and nurses who make assumptions about your partners, decisions, and lifestyle, your access is limited. Considering the factors that limit people's access clarifies the connection between reproductive issues and a host of other social issues.

Accessibility is a key concern to disability activists. Our physical environments are built to serve the needs of able-bodied people, but there is no reason that they couldn't be built differently. Access to reproductive services could be improved with better public transit. Access could be improved by universal health care, multilingual staff and culturally appropriate services, and health care policies that disregard immigration status. It could be improved by education about diverse relationships and families. While these solutions won't always be easy or cheap to implement, they are not rocket science.

The third word, "justice," means including the bigger picture. Looking at the above examples, we need to fight not just for access to health services, but for a world free of racism and discrimination. We need to dismantle centuries-old systems of colonialism and white supremacy, and establish relationships based on equity rather than exploitation. We need societies in which people with a variety of bodies, genders, and relationships can thrive. Historically—and still today—women, LGBTQ people, Indigenous people, people of colour, and disabled people have had less power in society. People with less money have had less power than people with more. People in richer countries, particularly in Western Europe and North America, have had power over people living in poorer ones. Justice means improving access and ensuring consent, while also addressing overarching power relationships.

Sometimes it's harder to see imbalances of power if we just look at the present. So to think about justice, we also need to look to the past. For example, in Australia, New Zealand, the United States, and Canada, we cannot truly support Indigenous youth in accessing their reproductive rights without addressing the legacy of boarding and residential schools and responding to broader calls for decolonization. In the United States, understanding why the state has particularly targeted the reproduction of black women means looking to histories of slavery as a foundation on which the country was built. To understand contemporary examples of sterilization abuse, it is useful to look at how sterilization practices have played out in the past. In other words, justice means thinking about reproductive issues in a bigger context—a world marked by inequities and power imbalances.

Together, consent, access, and justice are essential for building a movement that is rooted in people's rights and autonomous decision-making abilities—a movement that allows us to imagine a more radical meaning for the term "pro-choice."

2

MAKING
ABORTION
LEGAL

I N THE SPIRIT of the personal being political, let me share some of my story. I have been lucky enough to have never needed an abortion. I say lucky not because there should be any shame associated with this simple medical procedure, but because getting an abortion can still be a trying process. Often unnecessarily. One in three women will have an abortion in their lifetime, so the odds are good that I might need one in the future. In any case, it is more than likely that a friend and or family member will.

One time, in my early twenties, I thought I might be pregnant. My period was over a week late. I never doubted that if I were pregnant, I would have an abortion. I had just finished university. I was juggling two part-time jobs that barely paid the bills. I had recently discovered circus training, and I was doing a lot of this intensely physical work. I wasn't excited about having to stop. I had a committed partner, but our relationship was still quite new and I didn't feel like having a baby was really an option. In other words, it just wasn't a good time.

Even though I was sure that I would terminate the pregnancy, I resisted taking a pregnancy test. I did not want to be pregnant, and I did not want to go through the trials of getting an abortion. Even in Canada—a country that does not have laws regulating abortion—I knew that seeking one out would not be straight-forward. I have taken the morning-after pill on a few occasions, after momentary lapses in judgment and broken condoms. This is a simple over-the-counter medication. But I knew the way that pharmacists looked at me when I asked for it. Getting an abortion would be worse. I had seen several friends try to access abortion services. In the province of Nova Scotia, where I lived at the time, there can be significant wait times. Medical staff repeatedly question you about your decision, and you are forced to reiterate that you choose abortion over adoption or having and keeping a child. The hospital where the procedure is offered is a site of frequent anti-abortion protests. You have to make your way through a gamut of older white male protesters holding graphic photos and attempting to shame you. Under these conditions, many women suffer through the experience in silence and alone.

So I waited anxiously. I checked my underwear every time I went to the washroom, hoping for blood. I ate heaps of parsley, since I had heard that its high levels of vitamin C would encourage a pregnancy not to take. I consulted an herbalist friend and a tat-tered old feminist health zine about other safe alternative methods. And I waited. I was consumed by the situation for what seemed like weeks, before giving in and buying a pregnancy test. My part-ner waited on the couch in our dark basement apartment while I peed on the stick. Thankfully, it was negative. But I was stressed out for days until I finally had a period, over two weeks late.

ACCESS AND CONTROL

I tell this story not because it is particularly unique or interest-ing. After all, despite the stress the situation caused, I wasn't even pregnant. I tell it because it was an entirely normal situation. Most women will at some point experience the fear of an unwanted pregnancy. Many of those women will in fact be pregnant. I once worked at a university women's centre, where people would disclose intimate details or come looking for advice. So I have heard a lot of these stories. Teenaged single girls have these experiences. So do middle-aged women, married women, women who already have kids, and queer and trans people from a diversity of backgrounds. Though no two stories are exactly the same, these situations are always complicated and stressful for the people involved.

Which brings me to the second reason I tell this story. It highlights how the stigma surrounding abortion and the barriers to getting one can make being unintentionally pregnant even more difficult. This is true in countries where abortion is legal and in countries where it isn't. Of course, the consequences are more severe wherever safe, legal abortions aren't available. Societal pressures and draconian laws make a decision that may be personally straightforward unnecessarily painful. You may get a strong message that even though you *can* have an abortion, it really isn't okay.

A 2015 poll in the United States shows that only a slim majority—51 percent of Americans—believe that abortion should be legal in all or most cases.[1] Likewise, a 2012 poll indicates that only 49 percent of Canadians believe that an abortion should be available whenever a person decides they want one. (Only 6 percent, though, believe it should not be permitted under any circumstances.)[2] Organizations including the United Nations and the World Health Organization have affirmed the importance of safe, legal abortion. It is essential to ensuring women's health and human rights. But public opinion has not yet caught up.

Sometimes you'll hear anti-abortion advocates say that having an abortion is traumatic for women. But having a baby can be pretty traumatic too, particularly if it is an unwanted pregnancy. And abortions need not be traumatic, though added stigma and barriers can make the experience more emotionally trying.

Anti-abortion activities, and policies that dictate who can access legal abortions, are part of a bigger patriarchal project. They serve to control the bodies of women and trans people, often in support of other political interests. The stigma against those who need abortions, and policies that range from mandatory ultra-sounds and minimum wait times to jail sentences for accessing the procedure, are in large part intended to shame women and trans people for having sex at all. This affects even those who won't ever need an abortion.

All you have to do is turn on the TV or flip through a magazine to see that women are sexualized at every opportunity. In our culture women are valued primarily for their sexual attractiveness. But women are still not allowed to control their own sexuality and reproduction—this is supposed to remain the domain of men. Women are expected to take the "advice" of comedian Amy Schumer:

> Ask your doctor if birth control is right for you. Then ask your boss if birth control is right for you. Then ask your boss to ask his priest if birth control is right for you. Find a boy scout and see what he thinks. Tap a mailman on the shoulder ... then ask him if birth control is right for you.

The consequences of patriarchal thinking and restrictive abortion laws are not abstract. People die as a result of policies that prevent them from having control over their bodies. In 2008, an estimated 21.6 million women, 85 percent of whom were in countries of the Global South, underwent unsafe abortion procedures worldwide.[3] These abortions were often performed by people without the necessary qualifications or skills, or were self-induced. They may have taken place in unhygienic or dangerous conditions without post-abortion care. And they led to tens of thousands of deaths. Methods of inducing DIY abortions range from inserting long, sharp objects (like knitting needles or coat hangers) into the cervix, using chemicals (like bleach or detergent) or medication, vigorous abdominal massage, and herbal methods.[4] In general, the more invasive methods are more likely to be successful—and to be dangerous. Risks include heavy bleeding and blood poisoning, both of which can lead to death.

Complications from Unsafe Abortions

The World Health Organization estimates that eight women die every hour from the complications of unsafe abortions. Most illegal abortions are carried out in unsafe conditions. Complications include

- hemorrhage (profuse bleeding)
- sepsis (triggered by infection)
- peritonitis (tissue inflammation)
- trauma to cervix, vagina, uterus, and abdominal organs

Source: World Health Organization, "Unsafe Abortion: The Preventable Pandemic," journal paper, Sexual and Reproductive Health 4, www.who.int.

People have unsafe abortions for a variety of reasons. The chief one is lack of access to safe, legal abortions. Although 98 percent of countries permit abortion in order to save a woman's life, only 67 percent allow it to preserve physical health. Less than half permit abortion in case of rape or incest. Abortion procedures are only legal on request in 28 percent of countries.[5]

So in most of the world, the legal fight for abortion rights remains central to the struggle for abortion access. According to Women on Waves, about 25 percent of the global population lives in places with extremely restrictive abortion laws. Abortion is prohibited completely or allowed only when the woman's life is at risk in countries as diverse as Ireland, Mexico, the Philippines, Madagascar, and Afghanistan. In some countries, abortion is allowed to preserve the health of the mother or for socio-economic reasons. This can create a grey area in which abortion providers are unclear about when they can legally perform the procedure. Even in places where abortion is legal for any reason—as in much of Europe, Canada, the United States, Cuba, South Africa, Australia,

Nepal, and Vietnam—there are still legal and political challenges to abortion access.

ABORTION LAWS THEN

The landscape of abortion laws is constantly changing. In many places, the struggles of women and others have resulted in real gains for reproductive rights. Collective organizing and individual acts of defiance have challenged restrictive laws. Their successes are evidence that change is possible. But the changing legal landscape also has a downside. In countries where the fight for legal abortion rights is mostly historical, the efforts of anti-abortion groups threaten the status quo. Whatever legal situation our countries are in, we have a good deal to learn from each other's struggles.

We usually think of the decriminalization of abortion as a recent phenomenon. But in many places, it is actually its criminalization that is new. In much of Western Europe and North America, laws prohibiting abortion were only implemented in the nineteenth century. Previously, midwives and other healers had provided abortions and birth control techniques with little legal interference. Britain passed its first anti-abortion laws in 1803. Abortion was criminalized in France with the introduction of the Napoleonic Code in 1804. France occupied much of Europe during this time, and this code had a strong influence on the development of laws elsewhere. Abortion was made illegal across all Canadian provinces by 1869 and all U.S. states by 1880.

It wasn't until 1869—*after* many places had enshrined anti-abortion policy in law—that Pope Pius IX declared that the soul enters the human at conception.[6] So although we tend to think of opposition to abortion as religiously motivated, at the time these laws were enacted the motivations were more explicitly political.[7] University-trained male doctors were trying to establish medicine as a professional discipline. But remember how little their methods resembled anything we would now think of as "science." This push had more to do with establishing control than anything else. It was accompanied by an attempt to eliminate midwives and other female healers, and with them, female-centric practices like abortion.[8]

At the same time, first-wave feminism was beginning to take root. Movements for women's suffrage and other rights were emerging. One way male-controlled governments tried to prevent women from taking political action was by preventing "voluntary motherhood." That meant restricting access to abortion and contraceptives.[9] The nineteenth century also saw the rise of capitalism and industrialization. This economic system relied on some women to do unpaid household work and on others to become workers. This system, too, motivated state intervention into the reproductive lives of women.

The desire to control reproduction was also linked to political concerns about population growth. In colonial countries like the United States and Canada, white settler women were encouraged to have more babies and discouraged from accessing contraception and abortion. Encouraging white women to have babies was seen as one way to prevent "race suicide."[10] In the context of settler colonialism, encouraging the growth of white populations (while using sterilization campaigns to prevent Indigenous people and people of colour from having children) was one way to firmly establish the nations and to continue to dominate the land's Indigenous peoples.[11] Control over reproduction was a tool in the violent process of building a nation-state.

Similarly, Germany had begun to loosen its abortion laws in 1926. But Adolf Hitler's Nazi government, as part of the project of building an Aryan race, made it illegal to provide abortions to white women.[12] The will of individual women about what happened to their bodies was seen as expendable for grander—and often racist—political purposes.

The impact of these laws on people who needed abortions was similar to the impact of restrictive abortion laws today. Some women were likely discouraged from having abortions or using contraceptives. Others were simply prevented from getting them safely. People who did have abortions had them secretly and underground, away from the public eye. For this reason, it is difficult to accurately estimate the number of abortions performed before legalization. But in the United States, the number ranged from 200,000 to 1.2 million per year during the 1950s and 1960s. In the United Kingdom, it was (conservatively) estimated in 1964 that between 50,000 and 100,000 illegal abortions took place annually. In Canada, an estimated 35,000 to 120,000 abortions were illegally performed every year during the 1960s.[13]

It is also hard to find out who had an abortion and to learn their stories. Anyone who sought or provided an abortion had to be secretive. The stories we do have show that people accessing underground abortions came from diverse backgrounds.[14] Married women had abortions when their contraception failed and they felt for emotional or financial reasons that they could not have another child. Single women who got pregnant (at a time when even information about birth control was often illegal) were forced to decide between having the procedure or facing the stigma of giving birth to a child out of wedlock. No doubt women from higher social classes would have had better access to black market contraceptives and underground abortions. But women seeking these services spanned all social classes.

Finding someone to perform an abortion was a challenging obstacle. Self-induced abortions were common. Trish Hooper, an avid horseback rider, recalled trying to induce her own abortion in the United States at the age of nineteen:

> That day, I asked the man in charge to get my grandfather's horse ready for me with English saddle. He tried to steer me onto something gentler, but I stuck with my choice.... My idea was ride as fast as possible and fall off at a good place where surely I would be knocked out of being pregnant. We careened down towards the bay and as we passed the waterfall across the road I pulled the big horse up abruptly. He reared and down I went, hitting the ground hard.[15]

Nurses and midwives frequently performed abortions, as did some medical doctors. People with limited or questionable training, like waitresses and factory workers, did too. Sometimes they did so out of a genuine concern for the people they were working for. But just as often, providing abortions was a moneymaking venture. In Canada, the cost of an illegal abortion during the Great Depression was between C$150 and C$600—a significant amount for many people even today, but an astronomical fee at the time. In the United Kingdom, the cost of an abortion in the mid-1960s was between £100 and £150. In the United States, abortion providers charged upwards of US$1,000 during the 1960s.[16] To shield themselves from the law, abortion providers ensured that women came to them alone in secretive locations. Some women reported being blindfolded, having to use a password, or getting picked up in a car by a stranger. Fran Moreland Johns recounted being told to meet her provider alone:

He said[,] "If it looks like anyone might be watching or following you, the deal is off and there will be no second chance." I stood in front of the Loews Grand Theater that day in the icy February rain, as alone as I had ever been in my life, waiting for a black 1952 Buick sedan. Barney [the provider] pulled up, quickly reached back and opened the rear door, and pulled off as soon as I was halfway in. He handed me a musty, blue-flowered bandana, folded into a blindfold. "Tie this around your eyes," he said, "and sit in the middle of the seat. Have you got the money?"[17]

Connie Bryson recounted that during her illegal abortion in Brooklyn in 1953, she was told by her doctor not to yell out, to avoid police raids:

He gave me no anesthesia of any kind: no shot, no pills, not even an aspirin. There was a reason why he didn't give me painkillers: he wanted me to suffer, and he wanted to humiliate me. But I didn't cry out. I didn't make any noise at all. When he was finished, he forced me to look at the "product" of the procedure—blood and bits of tissue floating in a porcelain basin—and he warned me to stay away from boys. He then told me that I had a beautiful body, and then he sexually molested me. I still didn't scream.[18]

This kind of shaming and assault was a common part of the illegal abortion experience for many women. So was an incredible amount of physical pain. Anaesthesia was rarely used, and adequate precautions were rarely taken against infection or uncontrolled bleeding. Marie recounted the aftermath of her abortion in 1957:

The next day the pain started. The cramps were terrible—unlike anything I had ever experienced. After about two days of severe cramping, I began to hemorrhage and did miscarry. I remember going to the bathroom and having blood and clots just pour out of me. The blood was very dark, almost black. There was blood all over the bathroom floor. It was frightening . . . I had been told not to call a doctor. I was afraid that a doctor would call the police and I would go to jail. My roommate kept arguing that they wouldn't put me in jail, but I was sure they would. Not only had I done something illegal, but I had been driven there by a gangster. How much more illegal could it get?[19]

Marie eventually saw a doctor, but the scarring from the infection was so bad that she wasn't able to get pregnant again. Her experience was not uncommon. Frequently, if they suffered from complications, women were too afraid of legal and social consequences to seek help.

And the women quoted here were the lucky ones. They lived to tell the tale. In the United States, an estimated 5,000 people died from the procedure annually in the years before *Roe v. Wade*. In the

United Kingdom, records show that 160 women died from unsafe abortions from 1961 to 1963. In Canada, 4,000 to 6,000 women are estimated to have died from illegal abortion between 1926 and 1947, usually as a result of infection, hemorrhaging, drug poisoning, or embolisms. A newspaper report from 1970 estimated that 2,000 Canadian women died from unsafe abortions every year, with 20,000 being hospitalized due to complications.[20] Forced underground, women put their lives at risk in order to end their pregnancies.

In much of Europe, Canada, and the United States, restrictions on abortion and birth control were challenged in the radically charged environment of the 1960s. Underground abortion services and vocal demands for legal access became more common. Feminists took notice of the continued risk to women's lives. Using tactics ranging from letter-writing and petitions to radical guerilla presentations, they began a wave of protest calling for the complete decriminalization of abortion. With the sexual revolution, societal codes and stigma around premarital sex were loosening. Support for more widely available contraception and legal abortion gained ground.

By 1960, the birth control pill was available in Canada. But it could be legally prescribed only for regulating menstruation, not for birth control. Condoms were available for purchase, though kept out of sight, at many drugstores. A pharmacist in Toronto was convicted for selling condoms as late as 1960. By the end of the decade, the feminist call for access to contraception won out. In 1965 married couples were legally allowed to use the pill for birth control in the United States. In 1967, the United Kingdom allowed birth control advice on medical or social grounds for both married and unmarried individuals. In France, contraception was legalized in 1967. The Canadian government passed amendments to the Criminal Code that decriminalized contraception in 1969. In Spain, though, contraception was not permitted until 1978.

Restrictions on abortion also began to be loosened, though not nearly as completely. In Canada, the amendment to decriminalize

Historical Activism for Abortion Rights

National Women's Liberation Movement Conference: After a student at Ruskin College, Oxford, faced laughter for suggesting a history conference include women's history, the first of eight women's liberation conferences took place in 1970. Attendees discussed a vibrant contemporary rights movement. The conference's demands included free contraception and abortion on demand, alongside equal pay, educational opportunities, and free childcare. Later conferences demanded legal and financial independence, freedom from discrimination, and an end to sexual violence and violence against women.

Abortion Caravan: In 1970, the Vancouver Women's Caucus organized a cross-country protest tour for abortion on demand. Driving a convoy including a rooftop coffin representing deaths from unsafe abortions, they left Vancouver for the capital of Ottawa, gathering supporters and hearing stories. The caravan met a delegation from the east in Ottawa. A dramatic two-day protest included a massive theatrical funeral. Over thirty women chained themselves to seats in the House of Commons, causing chaos. Police removed them with bolt cutters, one protester threw a water bomb, and the House was forcibly adjourned for the first time in its history.

Jane Collective: Alarmed by dangerous and expensive illegal abortions by untrained people, a number of organizations helped women find safe abortion services. The Jane Collective, based in Chicago in the early 1970s, took matters into its own hands. It provided safe underground abortion services at an affordable cost. Advertising by word of mouth and operating out of two apartments, members eventually learned to perform abortions safely themselves. They provided over 11,000 illegal abortions over four years.

birth control also permitted abortions if a committee of doctors deemed a woman's life or health was in danger. However, the way this was interpreted by Therapeutic Abortion Committees varied widely. Some hospital committees approved nearly all requests; others denied requests made on the same grounds.[21] This created an inequitable situation. Access to abortion was largely a matter of luck.

Meanwhile, people found ways to get around the law. Abortion tourism—travelling to a place where abortion is more easily available—was common wherever abortions were illegal. In Europe, Geneva and Naples were known as cities with more accessible abortion services and extensive underground networks. Women travelling from abroad would be met at the train station and connected to midwives and other providers.[22] In Canada, women often travelled to clinics illegally operated by Henry Morgentaler. Following the 1973 *Roe v. Wade* decision, Canadian women travelled south of the border to obtain the procedure. Of course, this was often expensive and logistically difficult, as some hospitals had local residency requirements. Some U.S. doctors who were particularly committed to reproductive rights would waive fees or residency requirements. But overall, this type of access was available only to the privileged.[23]

A combination of political organizing and court battles led to eventual decriminalization of abortion in these countries. The specific circumstances differ. In the United Kingdom, the Conference of Cooperative Women passed a resolution in favour of legal abortions in 1934. The Abortion Law Reform Association—which aimed to change abortion laws—was formed in 1936. Against this backdrop of grassroots calls for reforms, Dr. Alec Bourne provided an abortion to a fourteen-year-old who was suicidal after being raped by a group of soldiers. Though abortion was illegal even in such dire circumstances, Bourne argued in court that an abortion was necessary to protect the mental health of the young woman. The case laid the groundwork for performing abortions to protect mental health.[24] This allowed women who could afford the cost of a psychiatrist to access abortions. Many others still had to resort to dangerous illegal abortions.

Throughout the 1950s and 1960s, U.K. feminist organizations, led by the Abortion Law Reform Association, continued to gain support for liberalization. Recognizing the public health risk posed by botched illegal abortions, a member of Parliament introduced a private member's bill to make abortion legal. The result was the Abortion Act of 1967. This law did not technically legalize abortions so much as provide a legal defence to those who had them. The law remains in place today in the United Kingdom, everywhere except Northern Ireland. It requires two doctors to consent to the procedure, and specifies that abortions can take place only in hospitals or government-approved clinics.

In the United States, expanded public conversation about abortion is often dated to a Planned Parenthood conference in 1955.

By 1970 the states of Hawaii, Alaska, New York, and Washington had legalized abortion. But it was a single pregnant woman named Norma L. McCorvey who challenged laws prohibiting abortion on a national level. McCorvey attempted to access an illegal abortion but found that her provider had been shut down by police. She approached lawyers to help her with her case, and used the alias Jane Roe in court. The resulting 1973 Supreme Court ruling—known as *Roe v. Wade*—determined that based on the right to privacy enshrined in the U.S. constitution, laws prohibiting abortion were unconstitutional. The court allowed states to regulate abortion services to protect women's health and protect the viability of life. As a result, despite abortion being legal nationally, many individual states today significantly restrict abortion access.

That same year in Canada, Henry Morgentaler announced publicly that he had broken the law by performing five thousand abortions outside of hospitals and without committee approval in Canada. He also filmed himself performing an abortion and had it shown on television. His brazen disregard for the law earned him multiple arrests in Quebec, where three separate juries failed to convict him. Eventually a new Quebec government decided the abortion law was essentially unenforceable. Backed by feminist organizations, Morgentaler set up clinics across Canada, challenging the law as he went. After yet another arrest and yet another acquittal, his case went to the Supreme Court of Canada, where it was decided that the law criminalizing abortions violated the new Canadian Charter of Rights and Freedoms (enacted in 1982). In January 1988 Canada's abortion law was officially struck down.

Many countries—including France, India, Turkey, and Cuba—liberalized their abortion laws to various extents from the 1960s to the 1980s. The 1990s and early 2000s have seen many more countries liberalize their laws—including Australia, Benin, Bhutan, Cambodia, Chad, Colombia, Ethiopia, Guinea, Iran, Mali, Nepal, Niger, Portugal, St. Lucia, Swaziland, Switzerland, Thailand, and Togo.[25] The specific reasons for these changes varied. But in most cases it was vibrant movements for feminism and social change combined with increasing recognition of the health risks posed by underground abortions. Truly accessible abortion services may not yet have arrived, but many people around the world can now have abortions in safer circumstances than was previously possible.

In the United States, the number of abortion-related deaths per million live births fell from 40 in 1970 to 8 in 1976.[26] This enormous change took place within only three years of abortion being legalized. Most of the decline can be attributed to fewer deaths from illegal abortions. Some sources suggest that the risk of dying from an unsafe illegal abortion is several hundred times higher than the risk from a legal one. Legalization also allowed for research into safe and effective methods of delivering abortions, and for doctors to be properly trained to carry out the procedure.[27] History is clear: decriminalizing abortion saves lives.

ABORTION LAWS NOW

Progress has been made since the 1950s. But in many places, legal restrictions still prevent people from accessing abortion safely. Women on Waves lists 54 countries in which abortion is illegal, or allowed only to save a women's life. There are 13 in Latin America, 22 in sub-Saharan Africa, 10 in the Middle East and North Africa, 7 in Asia and the Pacific, and 2 in Europe. And recent changes have not always been positive. Between 1997 and 2010, Poland, El Salvador, and Nicaragua all made their abortion laws more restrictive.[28]

Making abortion illegal means that those needing an abortion face greater hardships and greater risks. People who can afford to still travel across borders to access abortion and contraception. For example, abortion services are restricted in most of Mexico; they are forbidden in all cases in 18 out of 31 Mexican states. However, abortions up to twelve weeks have been legal—and free—in Mexico City since 2007. Those who can travel from across the country to access the procedure. In Ireland, a Supreme Court decision in the 1980s established that the life of a fetus and the mother have equal value. Abortion is therefore legal only if a woman's life is at risk. But Ireland, a relatively wealthy country, is close to other European countries with more liberal laws. Most Irish people seeking abortions—about 4,000 annually—travel to the United Kingdom to obtain the procedure, often with the help of referral agencies. It costs between €1,130 and €2,500 to cover the flight and procedure. In Poland abortion is banned unless the pregnancy threatens the health or life of the mother, is a result of a criminal act (such as rape), or the fetus is seriously ill or damaged. Illegal abortions in Poland can be costly and unsafe. And in a country where tensions on the issue run high, they are subject to significant stigma. So women frequently travel to the United Kingdom, Germany, Austria, and the Netherlands to access the procedure.[29]

In European countries with restrictive abortion laws, death from abortion is rare. These countries are relatively wealthy, and in proximity to countries with less restrictive laws. Occasionally, however, the serious consequences of restricting abortion access become apparent. In Ireland in October 2012, Savita Halappanavar died from a deadly inflammatory condition. She had begun to miscarry and went to the hospital, begging to obtain an abortion. The fetus was already unviable, but a fetal heartbeat was still present. The abortion was denied. The woman's midwife told her that she could not have an abortion because Ireland is a Catholic country. Halappanavar's death set off a wave of protests. Government inquiries confirmed that the medical team privileged the unviable fetus over the mother's health. Halappanavar would likely have lived had the medical team provided the abortion. In theory, Irish law allows abortion to protect the health of the mother. But medical practitioners and people seeking abortions are unclear about when they can be performed without legal reprisal. As health writer Jodi Jacobson noted in the aftermath of Halappanavar's death, "This is the inevitable outcome of abortion bans. Women die."[30]

In Chile, a complete abortion ban disallows abortion even if the mother's life is at risk. Wealthier people can travel to Cuba, Argentina, or the United States. But these are long, costly journeys. The laws force most of those needing abortions underground. The result? In Chile, there is a high number of unsafe abortions, and abortion complications result in up to 40 percent of maternal deaths.[31]

In Chile, you can be jailed for providing or consenting to an abortion or inducing your own. The situation is similar in most of Mexico, where 679 women were reported or sentenced for the crime of abortion between 2009 to 2011—including some who swear they miscarried. In Northern Ireland in 2016, several woman faced charges for purchasing the abortion pill. One was a mother charged with providing the medication to her daughter. The women faced up to five years of jail time.[32]

Under laws like these, women fear legal reprisal. If they experience complications from unsafe abortions or even miscarriages, they are less likely to seek follow-up care. Doctors may also be unwilling to treat women suffering from complications. In Nicaragua, a woman died in hospital when doctors, shortly after a new abortion law came into effect, refused treatment for vaginal bleeding. Nicaraguan doctors also hesitate to treat conditions like HIV, malaria, and cancer during pregnancy. They fear reprisal if they inadvertently injure the fetus.[33]

Even where the procedure itself is allowed, legal limitations can prevent people from obtaining an abortion. In Mauritius, abortion is only legal when a woman's life is in danger, and the procedure must be approved by the Supreme Court. The process is so difficult and time-consuming that there are no reported cases of the procedure being carried out legally. In Zambia, a country without an abundance of doctors, a woman must get the consent of several doctors and a specialist before the procedure is allowed. In other cases, timelines determine how late in a pregnancy a woman can access abortion. The time it takes to jump through bureaucratic hoops may mean that women miss this window of opportunity. In Turkey, where abortions are permitted up to ten weeks, the law specifies that the procedure must be carried out by a gynecologist, who are few and far between.[34]

Places with more liberal laws also experience legal threats. In the United Kingdom, the 1967 Abortion Act has been challenged by anti-abortion organizations and politicians. In 2008 there was an unsuccessful attempt to decrease the timeframe in which abortions could be legally carried out. At the time of writing, Canadian members of Parliament have introduced more than forty-five private members' bills or motions to recriminalize or limit abortion access. One government bill sought to criminalize abortions except to save the woman's life or health. The defeat of such measures hasn't stopped anti-abortion politicians and groups from trying. This is in part because of the success of such initiatives in the United States. While the *Roe v. Wade* ruling stands on a federal level, several states have introduced legislation that makes abortion extremely difficult to access. These efforts will likely be bolstered by the 2016 election of U.S. president Donald Trump.

Where abortion is legal, anti-abortion initiatives fall into a couple of categories. The most obvious approach is to limit the circumstances in which people can legally have an abortion. These restrictions usually call for abortions to be available only to save the woman's life. Other bills would criminalize late-term abortions, or allow abortions only with the referral of a doctor or multiple doctors. A related approach is to prevent most abortions from being covered by government health care plans. Or to create such specific, demanding regulations about where and when abortions can be performed that few providers can meet them.

Parental consent laws, common in some U.S. states, can make it difficult for teens, especially if they have abusive or hostile parents, to access the procedure. Comedian Sarah Silverman points out the irony: "Much like the pro-lifers, I believe in protecting the child—when she's being forced to have a baby at fourteen." Mandatory consideration periods between the initial clinic visit and the procedure prolong the amount of time one is forced to deal with an unwanted pregnancy.

When presented as a package, these kinds of laws can make abortion practically impossible to access. Clinics close as a result of complex legislation. People have to travel farther, which is made more difficult by mandatory consideration periods that require multiple visits. Thus travel costs, and the inconvenience of taking time off school or work, are multiplied. When it takes longer, it becomes harder to obtain abortions early in pregnancy and more likely that the procedure will be delayed beyond legal timelines.

Another common strategy is to attack abortion access less directly, or couch anti-abortion goals in the language of women's rights or religious freedom. These measures appropriate social justice goals for other ends. For example, in places like Poland, Turkey, Canada, and the United States, there have been efforts to introduce "conscience clauses." These clauses would protect medical professionals if they refuse to perform procedures that run counter to their religious beliefs. Of course, professional ethics codes often already allow this, as long as referrals are made, so that medical professionals do not violate their obligations to their patients. Conscience clause initiatives would remove the duty to refer. They can also prevent institutions from considering the willingness to per-form a given procedure in making hiring or firing decisions. That means, in theory at least, that an abortion clinic might be forced to hire a person who refused to perform abortions or to support women's decisions to access them.

Even more insidious are bills that frame a desire to limit abor-tion rights in the language of women's rights. Several initiatives would give rights to the fetus under the guise of protecting preg-nant women. In the United States, the Unborn Victims of Violence Act, enacted in 2004, is couched in that language. It allows separate charges to be laid for the fetus when a pregnant woman is violently attacked. The law explicitly states that it cannot be used against someone who has had an abortion. But critics maintain that its language could be the basis of a challenge to *Roe v. Wade*. The Act has also been invoked to punish pregnant women suffering from

addictions. They end up in jail rather than in appropriate health care facilities.[35] Efforts to pass similar legislation in Canada, such as the proposed Unborn Victims of Crime Act in 2008, have thus far been unsuccessful.

In Canada and the United Kingdom, the issue of sex-selective abortions has recently been used. A Canadian member of Parlia-ment introduced a motion in 2012 aiming, according to his website, to "stop gendercide." Fetuses that would be born female, he claimed, are more likely to be aborted. This was a clear effort to frame the motion as one in support of women's rights. A similar attempt was made to ban sex-selective abortions in the United Kingdom in 2015. Evidence from the Department of Health, though, showed that the practice is not widespread.[36]

These initiatives play on racial stereotypes and fears that immi-grants—particularly from India—are more likely to want male chil-dren and to abort female ones. They make use of an overarching cultural storyline: women's rights are safe in white communities, but women of colour and women in Asian countries need to be saved from misogynist men and cultures. In the context of legal changes designed to chip away at women's right to terminate pregnancy, this is an ironic claim. There are cultural, social, and economic reasons that an Asian immigrant might prefer a male child. Wealthy white Westerners are also known to practise sex selection. They might, though, be more likely to practise it through expensive prenatal techniques rather than abortion.[37] There are similarities in tactics between those fighting for legislation on sex-selective abortion and the broader anti-abortion movement. So it seems clear that the concern is more motivated by a desire to restrict abortion access than by gender inequality.[38]

In India, an Act was passed in 1994 to stop the abortion of fetuses that would be female at birth. Inspectors visit health care providers to enforce the law. But many providers have stopped providing abortions altogether. They have no way of knowing if their patients are pursuing sex-selective abortion or not.[39] In India, the United Kingdom, and Canada, this issue could be addressed in more constructive ways. Educational initiatives could combat sexist and patriarchal attitudes. More social power could be given to women, immigrants, and people of colour. The motions on sex-selective abortions are part of a trend among anti-abortion activists to mask their objectives and frame their issues in the language of gender or racial justice.

Many of the proposed laws that would restrict abortion access don't pass. But their existence still fuels anti-abortion sentiment, with practical consequences. In Turkey, for example, a law was proposed in 2012 that would allow doctors to refuse to perform the procedure on grounds of conscience and would implement a mandatory consideration time for women. Thousands of activists staged demonstrations against the law across the country, and it was dropped.[40] The effects of the government's anti-abortion stance were still felt, however. Reports from women's organizations suggest that women accessing abortion services were treated badly by hospital staff. After the law was proposed, some women underwent abortions without anaesthesia. Some hospitals implemented reporting systems in which fathers were informed that their daughters were pregnant. In a country where sex outside of

Activism for Abortion Rights Today

I Was Born to Fly is a youth-driven organization in Nicaragua. Based in the municipality of Condega, it hosts workshops on reproductive rights in rural communities, encouraging participants to share their knowledge with others. Building on a history of revolutionary feminist organizing in Nicaragua (a legacy challenged by conservative governments and a complete abortion ban in recent years), I Was Born to Fly educates young people about sexual, reproductive, and citizenship rights for women.

The Abortourism Travel Office is an entirely fictional travel agency created by Hungarian activists. It urges abortion seekers to "soak up the Spanish sunshine and buy up the Spanish pharmacies' contraceptive pill stock!" Although you can't book travel through this agency, its creative ads and web presence highlight different countries' laws around contraception and abortion—and the ridiculousness of having to travel across borders to obtain basic medical care.

Miles is a Chilean organization that advances the conversation around sexual and reproductive rights and works to change oppressive laws. Although Miles deals with serious issues, it is not afraid to add a touch of humour and shock value. In satire aimed at the insanity of the current abortion ban in Chile—where only accidental abortions are legal—a series of YouTube videos shows women giving advice about how to induce their own abortions. One advises women to buy high-heeled shoes, slice the heel, then go outside and trip against a fire hydrant. A woman can then point to the broken shoe as proof that the miscarriage was accidental.

marriage is widely frowned upon, this is a patriarchal and stigmatizing move. By 2015, 34 out of 37 hospitals refused to provide non-emergency terminations altogether.[41]

The situation in Turkey illustrates how government policy and cultural stigma can work hand in hand. Laws may prescribe fines and jail time to dissuade people from providing or accessing abortions. Cultural attitudes, though, may determine how accessible abortion is on the ground. Significant legal and cultural barriers remain for people who need an abortion. However, people around the world continue to fight for safe, legal abortion access.

A recent motion introduced in Canada asked the government to affirm that "a woman's right to choose abortion is a fundamental question of equality and human rights, both in Canada and around the world."[42] While this motion did not pass, it is an encouraging sign that some politicians and lawmakers—especially when backed with grassroots support—will go to bat for abortion rights. Other advocates are challenging cultural attitudes as a first step to changing oppressive laws.

Legal battles can keep those who need abortions from being criminalized. But laws can only do so much if the environments in which people seek out abortions are hostile. Even where abortion is legal, people are still fighting for supports needed to allow access to the full scope of reproductive decision-making.

3

MAKING
ABORTION
ACCESSIBLE

I N MANY countries today, the laws allow people who have abortions to do so at the hands of a trained medical professional, usually in hospitals or abortion clinics, with little risk. But legal wins do not always end the struggle for access. I was a baby when abortion was decriminalized in Canada, but I have still found it necessary to attend dozens of rallies and protests. I have held red coat hangers and participated in mock funerals to draw attention to the deaths that still result from unsafe abortions.

Many of the barriers to accessing abortion are barriers to accessing health care generally. Prohibitively expensive fees. Inadequate health insurance. Stigma and misunderstanding faced by groups like LGBTQ individuals. Limited clinic hours that don't match the schedules of shift workers. Or simply the unavailability of adequate medical facilities.

Typically these barriers hit already marginalized communities the hardest. People who can't afford to manage debt, take time off work to go to a clinic, or find resources to access stigma-free care bear the brunt. And as a result of colonization, traditional knowledge and practices for culturally appropriate abortion methods have often been lost.

Reproductive Justice
and the LGBTQ Community

Let's dispel the myth that the LGBTQ community doesn't care about reproductive issues because its members don't have to worry about unwanted pregnancy. LGBTQ people may end up having intercourse with someone of the opposite sex for any number of reasons. Also, trans women can get female partners pregnant, and trans men can become pregnant. In all of these cases, access to safe abortion services may be vital.

The right to have and parent children also comes to the fore. Diverse family arrangements are common in the LGBTQ community. But health care, legal, and social systems rarely support co-parenting, single parents, extended family networks, and so on. Adoption by same-sex or queer couples is legal in some places, but they continue to face stigma by adoption agencies. The high cost of assisted reproductive technologies also affects this community particularly.

The fight for LGBTQ liberation shares many common goals with the fight for reproductive justice. The religious right assumes that sexual activity is acceptable only if reproduction and childbirth are possible. This means no contraception, abortion, or sex between people of the same sex. In this context, the sex lives, gender identities, and desires of LGBTQ people are considered illegitimate and pushed underground.

The U.S.-based Causes in Common coalition encourages allies in both movements to sign a pledge committing to sexual and reproductive freedom. The right's agenda makes one thing clear. Sexual liberation and reproductive liberation are intimately related. One cannot be fully achieved without the other.

Because the procedure is politicized, accessing an abortion presents particular barriers. Politicians and members of the public may hold anti-abortion attitudes, so they don't often make widely available abortion services a priority. As governments across the globe slash budgets for health care and social services, politically controversial services are easy targets. And there's the impact of the religious right. Even where abortion is legal, grassroots initiatives continue to oppose clinic closures, challenge stigma, and support people in accessing the services.

FINDING AN ABORTION CLINIC

These days, the biggest barrier to accessing an abortion may be finding a place to get one. It is a relatively simple procedure. But many places—even if they have liberal laws on paper—make people jump through hoops in order to access it. To get accurate information, you have to navigate anti-abortion attitudes—among hospital staff, medical practitioners, and the general public.

Take the example of Canada. This country is often held up as a place with reasonable access. Abortion has been decriminalized and there are no restrictions as to why you might get one. But a 2006 Canadians for Choice study found that only 15.9 percent of Canadian hospitals offered accessible abortion services, a decrease of 2 percentage points from just a few years earlier.[1] Most of the hospitals that did provide abortions were in urban areas in the south of the country. People living outside of these zones had minimal access.

For many years, abortion was entirely unavailable in the province of Prince Edward Island. If you needed the procedure, you'd have to travel to a hospital over 300 kilometres away in Halifax, Nova Scotia. And at that hospital in Halifax, it's very difficult to get information about accessing abortions. A Canadians for Choice researcher had to speak to six different people and leave a voicemail before getting the correct information.[2] Then there were conditions to have the out-of-province procedure covered by Prince Edward Island's provincial health insurance. You'd have to find a doctor who was willing to make a referral. On a small, socially conservative island, this could be a challenge. The doctor would have to deem the procedure medically necessary, and request that it be funded by the Department of Health and Social Services.

For years, grassroots organizations protested this hypocritical "anywhere but here" approach. Abortion Access Now PEI eventually took the provincial government to court. It argued that access to abortion was guaranteed under the Canadian Charter of Rights and Freedoms. In the face of the legal challenge, Prince Edward Island conceded in March 2016 that it would begin providing abortion services by the end of the year.

This case illustrates several of the barriers that limit access to abortions even where it is legal. You might have trouble getting your health insurance to pay for the procedure. Referrals from doctors—also a requirement in some U.S. states and many European countries—lengthen the amount of time you're dealing with an unwanted pregnancy. And the stigma you'll face even from professionals—including doctors and hospital staff whose job it is to provide these services—may make it hard to get accurate information or access a referral.

Then there is the question of why, in a country where the procedure is legal, abortion wouldn't be available in any well-equipped hospital. In places where it is illegal, it is obvious why people might travel long distances for an abortion. It is less clear why abortion tourism is alive and well in places with relatively liberal laws. But where abortion is legal, the geographic distribution of clinics is often sparse. Tunisia is held up as a model for women's rights in the Muslim world. Abortion has been legal there since 1973. But in recent years, there has been a decline in publicly provided abortion services. Residents of the south and northwest have complained that abortion services are no longer available in their area. In the United States, the National Abortion Federation notes that 87 percent of counties have no abortion providers. This number rises to 97 percent outside of urban centres.[3]

The regional lack of services most affects communities that are already marginalized. Travelling to obtain an abortion means days off work, childcare, hotel and transportation costs—not to mention medical costs. The time needed to travel may also mean that you have to wait longer to have an abortion. In addition, there may be mandatory wait times between the initial clinic visit and the actual procedure. And in some places, abortions are only available early in the pregnancy.

When clinics that provide abortion close, it often means the loss of other sexual and reproductive health care services as well. It is widely acknowledged, though, that the best way to reduce abortions is not to limit access. It is to provide sexual education and access to effective contraceptives. Clinic closures, then, are counterproductive.

Unfortunately, abortion is increasingly unavailable in many places. This trend is most apparent in the United States. Restrictive legislation aims to regulate abortion to the extent that access is practically impossible. This strategy is proving effective. Fifty U.S. abortion clinics closed permanently in 2014.[4]

In Texas in 2013, a law was passed that bans abortions after twenty weeks. It also requires that abortion clinics meet the same standards as hospital surgical centres. And doctors performing abortions at clinics must have admitting privileges at a nearby hospital. This type of restrictive legislation is known as a TRAP (targeted regulation of abortion providers) law. Similar laws are in place in many U.S. states. TRAP laws do not challenge the legality of abortion directly. But they impose unnecessary regulations on clinics, making it harder for abortion providers to keep their doors open. Supporters of the Texas bill claim that the law is designed to protect women. But the American College of Obstetricians and Gynecologists maintains that these requirements are unnecessary for providing most abortions safely.[5] At the time the bill passed, only five of Texas's forty-two abortion clinics met the law's standard.[6] A wave of clinic closures followed. As a result, many women in Texas face average wait times of up to twenty days, and have to travel far from home for the procedure.[7]

CUTS TO HEALTH CARE

To access safe abortions, or to address the complications of unsafe abortions, women must be able to access health care services in the first place. In the Global South and among Indigenous peoples in the Global North, traditional health care practices and knowledge systems have largely been replaced by Western systems. In a context of colonization and globalization, we can debate the relative benefits of Western medicine. But it is clear that access to Western medicine is often scarce.

For example, in both Canada and the United States, the health care systems available to Indigenous people are woefully inadequate.[8] This contributes to poor health outcomes in general. It also leads to a lack of access to reproductive health care in particular.[9] In India, Nepal, and Cambodia, abortion is legal on broad grounds. But most abortions are still performed in dangerous, unhygienic, or otherwise substandard conditions. In India, conditions in most public health care facilities are poor, and most abortion providers work in expensive, for-profit clinics. So only two-fifths of abortions are considered safe.[10]

In the Global South, Structural Adjustment Programs (SAPs) contribute to the desperate state of health care services. These programs of neoliberal or "free market" reforms have been forced upon developing countries by the World Bank and International Monetary Fund. Countries must accept them in order to access development assistance or renegotiate the terms of debt repayment. SAPs often call for wide-ranging changes in economic policy. Government funding for health care and other social services must often be removed. When people have to pay user fees, it's an additional barrier to accessing abortions or follow-up care.

Global Gag Rule

The Global Gag Rule, also known as the Mexico City Policy, is an intermittent U.S. policy. It bans organizations that receive U.S. development funding from providing or promoting abortions, even if the U.S. funds are not used for that purpose. It was first introduced by president Ronald Reagan in 1984, and was rescinded and reinstated by successive Democratic and Republican administrations. The Global Gag Rule had not been in effect under Barack Obama, but Donald Trump reinstated the policy during his first week in office. The international community, led by the Netherlands, introduced plans to set up an international safe abortion fund in response.

While the law is in effect, maternal health and family planning organizations are forced to make a choice. They can provide women with a full range of reproductive options that include abortion. Or they can receive funding from the U.S. government.

The effect of SAPs on health care is a catch 22. Communities were encouraged (and sometimes forced) to abandon traditional knowledge systems and health care practices. (As part of a struggle to reclaim them, Indigenous communities in Canada and the United States have been reviving Indigenous midwifery practices.[11]) But the systems that replaced traditional practices are inadequate at meeting people's needs. Services previously provided by the government are often provided by non-governmental organizations. Many NGOs rely on foreign aid for support. But foreign aid policies like the United States' Global Gag Rule—which restricts the use of U.S. development funds for abortions—often mean that those providing abortion services or referrals won't be funded.

The lack of affordable health care is a barrier in the Global North as well. According to Planned Parenthood, first-trimester abortions in the United States cost up to US$1,500; later-term abortions cost even more.[12] One advantage of abortion being legal is that it is more likely to be at least partially covered by health insurance programs. But some jurisdictions restrict insurance coverage for abortion. And particularly in places without comprehensive government-sponsored plans, many people lack access to health insurance altogether.

The United States is known for big divides among its classes when it comes to health care. The Affordable Care Act, also known as Obamacare, was introduced in 2010 in an effort to make health insurance more affordable. The policies still fall short of the universal health care plans that many countries have. And even this minimal coverage has been threatened by Donald Trump's administration. But nevertheless, anti-abortion organizations used the opportunity to protest changes that could allow greater abortion access. They have invoked the Hyde Amendment—a provision that forbids the use of U.S. federal funds to pay for abortions except in cases of rape, incest, or to save the mother's life. Although their arguments did not stop the Act from going ahead, twenty-five states have restricted coverage for abortion in insurance plans offered through the insurance marketplaces established by Obamacare.[13]

Few mainstream U.S. feminists have taken on the fight against the Hyde Amendment. It primarily affects low-income people who qualify for social assistance. It also affects those serving in the military, federal prison inmates, Native Americans, and others whose health care is paid for with federal funds. But it's a mistake to disregard abortion access for everyone, including people from marginalized communities. We're now seeing the broad consequences. A legal provision that originally restricted access for low-income individuals is now being felt across social classes.

I am lucky to live in a country that is renowned for its universal health care. Government-funded insurance pays for basic health care services—including, in most cases, abortion. But in recent years, many Western governments have aggressively pursued "austerity" agendas. They aim to reduce government budget deficits—usually by slashing services like health care. In Canada, this has resulted in the underfunding of several health services, abhorrently long wait times, and what many see as a gradual chipping away at public health care.

Cuts to health care inevitably include cuts to reproductive health care. So a struggle for reproductive justice must include a broader fight to protect an accessible, equitable health care system for all.

LACK OF ABORTION PROVIDERS

Too few doctors are trained, and willing, to provide abortions. Abortions are fairly simple, straightforward medical procedures. But most doctors have not learned how to provide them. In the United States, the American Medical Association's code of ethics allows medical students to opt out of performing abortions—and most do.[14] According to an article published in 2011, under 10 percent of family medicine residencies offered training in abortion. A 2009 article indicated that 25 percent of obstetricians and gynecologists received no formal training in providing abortions during their clerkships.[15] While many medical school programs discuss the ethics of abortion, little time is spent learning the procedure.

My friend Dr. Melissa Brooks is a recent graduate who now works as an obstetrician and gynecologist in Canada. She told me that there was little formal training on abortion in medical school. There are many competing demands on what to include in the curriculum, and politicized issues like abortion are likely to cause some pushback. So, she says, they tend to be conveniently left out.

Medical Students for Choice is one organization working to change this situation. It wants to destigmatize abortion among medical students and professionals and effect changes to curricula. This international organization also helps students and residents access training in abortion provision. But until abortion is included as part of core medical training, most medical students won't be exposed to this basic procedure.

"If you are a family doctor or any medical professional, you are going to encounter unplanned pregnancies. Knowing how to deal with it is part of caring for your patient," Melissa told me. Including abortion in the curriculum does more than just teach the procedure. "It gets rid of stigma. Many people have stereotyped ideas about the kinds of women seeking abortions. But if you spend some time in an abortion clinic, you learn that all kinds of women need abortions. Most women are at risk of needing an abortion at some point," Melissa says. This is reason enough to expose medical doctors to the procedure. One of the first people you'll encounter if you need an abortion is likely your family doctor. The doctor's response can make a big difference in how supported you'll feel throughout the process.

Medical professionals may also fear the consequences of providing abortions. In some cases, the fear is of being stigmatized in a community, especially in smaller, rural, or conservative areas. Most anti-abortion protesters do little more than pray and write letters to the editor. But doctors who provide abortions have learned to expect hate mail, and most prefer to keep a low profile. It was recently revealed that in Texas, training sessions for anti-abortion activists include explicit encouragement to harass and intimidate. They are taught to record licence plates, write down physical descriptions of patients and providers, and intimidate women into cancelling their appointments.[16] And the more extreme wings of the anti-abortion movement have at times resorted to outright violence.

In 2009, late-term abortion doctor George Tiller was murdered by an anti-abortion activist at a church service in Wichita, Kansas. Tiller was famous for using the slogan *Trust women*. Tiller's clinic had been firebombed in 1986, and he was shot in both arms in 1993. From 2009 to 2012, the U.S. National Abortion Federation counts eight additional instances of extreme violence aimed at providers or clinics, including arson and attempted murder.[17] In 2015, a gunman fired on a Planned Parenthood clinic in Colorado, killing three and wounding nine. That same year, there were four arson attempts and one violent break-in at Planned Parenthood clinics in the United States.[18]

This kind of extremism is seen elsewhere too. The Toronto clinic of Dr. Henry Morgentaler was firebombed in 1992. Canadian abortion providers have been attacked in Winnipeg and Hamilton. Abortion specialist Garson Romalis of Vancouver was attacked twice. He was shot in his home in 1994 and stabbed outside his clinic in 2000. Although Dr. Romalis continued to perform abortions until his death in 2014, he was accompanied by a bodyguard at all times.

In Australia in 2001, an extremist tried to burn a Melbourne clinic. Fifteen staff and twenty-six patients were inside. The attacker was unsuccessful, but he did murder the clinic's security guard. A 2009 firebombing of a medical clinic in Western Australia is also attributed to anti-abortion extremists. The clinic didn't actually provide abortions, but graffiti reading "baby killers" on the building was linked to the attacks.

Thankfully, these are relatively isolated incidents. But they impose a chill on reproductive health practitioners. It's not surprising that people aren't lining up to become abortion doctors. Protection is needed for those who do provide abortions. In response, some places have enforced bubble zone laws. They restrict protests in the areas immediately surrounding abortion clinics, hospitals, and doctors' homes. Laws of this kind exist in South Africa, the Australian state of Tasmania, the Canadian province of British Colombia, and the U.S. states of Colorado, Massachusetts, and Montana. They have been shown to drastically reduce the number of anti-choice protesters near clinics, helping abortion providers and those accessing them feel safer.

I asked Melissa why, knowing the risks and the extra effort to access the training, she would do this work. Her response was poignant: "I find it very rewarding. Most people think it must be sad. But if someone is in a situation they don't want to be in, and it takes a ten-minute procedure to change that, why wouldn't you? It's easy, it's safe, and you've probably changed the course of their life."

TACTICS OF THE RELIGIOUS RIGHT

In recent years, the religious right has become a significant cultural force. Its members, usually from Christian traditions, hold extremely conservative views on social issues. And they act on those views politically. The group is diverse, but its members typically oppose abortion and contraception, the teaching of evolution in schools, and LGBTQ rights. Their faces are familiar to anyone who has had slurs hollered at them while accessing an abortion clinic. And their views are sometimes used to justify violent attacks on abortion providers. The religious right is typically associated with the evangelical Christian movement in the United States. Its extremist values are being exported, including to Canada and Europe. Similar socially conservative, religiously motivated ideals also flourish elsewhere.

Certainly not all religious people fall into this category. Branches of most religions interpret their teachings much more liberally and progressively. Most of the American Jewish population supports legal abortion, regardless of political leanings.[19] People who practise Orthodox forms of Judaism tend to support abortion when there is a direct threat to the mother's life. Abortion is illegal in most Muslim countries, with the exception of Tunisia. While few Muslims encourage abortion, many Muslim scholars see abortion as permissible in the first four months of pregnancy, especially if there is a threat to the mother's life or health.[20]

Among Christians, several denominations—including the United Church of Christ, the Presbyterian Church, and the Evangelical Lutheran Church—take positions that support a fuller range of reproductive decisions. And even within denominations that take hard-line positions against abortion, there is a substantial movement for change. Unfortunately, however, this diversity of perspectives can get lost. The loudest religious voices are often those opposing abortion. In the United States, organizations like

Religious Organizations
for Reproductive Rights

Many people associate being religious with being anti-abortion. But religious adherents have diverse positions on reproductive rights. Here are a few examples of religious organizations open to broader conversations.

Catholics for Choice is an organization of Catholics who "disagree with the dictates of the Vatican on matters related to sex, marriage, family life and motherhood." It challenges the church hierarchy's narrow view of morality. The group first made headlines in 1984 when it published "A Catholic Statement on Pluralism and Abortion" in the *New York Times*. This move earned signatories a formal reprimand by the Vatican, and two nuns ended up leaving their order. The group publishes *Conscience* magazine, which explores reproductive rights, gender, sexuality, and feminism.

Muslim Sisters' Leadership Institute is a program of the Jahajee Sisters organization of Indo-Caribbean women. It aims to empower Muslim youth on issues of reproductive justice, Islamophobia, sex education, racism, sexism, and LGBTQ rights. In one initiative, youth create public service announcements and YouTube videos about their experiences. These videos address sexual and gender expectations for Muslim women and girls, Islamophobia, and sexual assault.

Religious Coalition for Reproductive Choice, a U.S.-based coalition of over twenty-five religious organizations, wants to change the impression that being religious means being against sex ed, contraception, and abortion care. Made up of Christian and Jewish faith groups, the coalition believes women should have the moral agency to make decisions about their own lives and reproduction. It supports research, education, and action, and offers tools to help youth leaders, activists, and religious leaders promote compassionate responses to the reproductive issues facing their communities.

Focus on the Family, the Alliance Defending Freedom, and the Family Research Council have significant political influence. And the religious right has become a powerful cultural force.

It is easy to imagine that the anti-abortion movement is primarily made up of elderly, church-going retirees with antiquated views. In other words, not a group that would have a major impact on wider cultural opinion. For example, the annual 40 Days for Life vigil in Halifax—anti-abortion protesters who set up shop outside the city's abortion-providing hospital twenty-four hours a day for forty days—is dominated by older white men. But this isn't an accurate picture of who makes up the anti-abortion movement.

Campaign Life, for example, is an anti-abortion organization that also opposes LGBTQ rights and stem cell research. It estimates that tens of thousands of people attended its 2014 March for Life in Canada's capital city of Ottawa. Many of them were

Catholic high school students who had been given the day off to attend. Campaign Life makes a point of engaging youth. It focuses political action on school boards, fighting progressive sexual and reproductive education.

In the past decade, anti-abortion activities on university campuses and in high schools have been encouraged by larger non-student organizations. I first became aware of this phenomenon when the Canadian Centre for Bio-Ethical Reform paid a visit to Saint Mary's University in Halifax. The organization, an offshoot of the Center for Bio-Ethical Reform in the United States, is famous for its graphic presentations. Designed for maximum shock value and placed where students cannot avoid running into them, they feature bloody close-ups of abortion procedures and compare abortions to the Holocaust and slavery. The so-called Genocide Awareness Project (GAP) was displayed at the University of British Columbia every year from 1999 to 2013. Reproductive rights organizations there claim that the posters are designed to spark hatred and conflict.

At Saint Mary's, the organization organized a public lecture. In the face of protests by local feminists, it was ultimately moved off campus. But nonetheless, the visit had the desired effect. The following year, when I was working at the university's Women Centre, an anti-abortion group applied to the student association for official recognition, including access to space and funding. Citing freedom of speech, the student association approved the request, even though the club's activities would likely cause conflict in the school. A similar story has been repeated across North America. Anti-abortion groups are becoming commonplace on campus.

Even more troubling is the way the movement co-opts the language of social justice to advance patriarchal goals. For example, preventing abortions is framed as preventing genocide. This language is designed to appeal to a generation steeped in the horrors of the Holocaust and taught to abhor the dehumanization that made slavery and segregation possible. But remember that the anti-abortion project does nothing to fight racism or anti-Semitism. Nor does it promote anti-oppression or any other social justice practices. During the Holocaust, people were sterilized under a eugenics law. Slavery in the United States relied on black women's procreative abilities. Both are examples of heavy-handed state control of reproduction, control that anti-abortion rhetoric only encourages.

This is why black reproductive justice leaders have been vocal in their opposition to the Genocide Awareness Project.[21] GAP uses these horrifying histories for its own ends. It does nothing to honour, respect, or remember them or to address their contemporary manifestations. Using language of justice, equality, and human rights is an appeal to youthful idealism. But the movement advocates for policies that would hurt women, the LGBTQ community, and marginalized people generally.

Concerned Women of America and REAL Women of Canada also ride on this trend, using the language of feminism. Describing themselves as a "pro-family, conservative women's movement," these organizations fight against issues including same-sex marriage, abortions, and labour unions. They uphold a paternalistic, patriarchal vision of a family unit. Universal childcare and pay equity, two uncontroversial goals of mainstream feminism, would go a long way to supporting families. But these issues don't make the cut.

Similar organizations, like Feminists for Life in the United States, do advocate for services that would make parenting easier. But they tend to reduce supporting women to supporting motherhood. And they don't support abortion, even in cases of rape or where mother's life or health is at risk. By framing themselves as caring about the advancement of women, these organizations have attracted media attention. They are often disturbingly represented as showing another side to feminism.

These tactics prey on weaknesses of the feminist movement. Take, for example, a recent trend in the United States, exemplified by the website BlackGenocide.org. Going a step further than the Genocide Awareness Project, it contends that a disproportionate number of abortions occur in the black community and that stopping abortion would be an issue of racial justice. But consider the context. Black women have histories of being involuntarily sterilized or coerced into taking dangerous long-term contraceptives. Legal scholar Dorothy Roberts argues that control over the reproduction of black women began with efforts to induce slave women to have more children. And that it has continued with efforts to limit the reproduction of black women as a means of population and social control. Reproductive control "has been a central aspect of racial oppression in America," she writes.[22]

By and large, the mainstream feminist community has failed to connect control over reproduction with racist and colonial interests. A single-issue, individualistic focus on abortion rights has prevailed. Angela Davis suggests that feminists have tended to blur the line between support for abortion rights and support for abortion per se. But many women of colour would prefer to have access to greater social, political, and economic power that would allow them to parent more children. They may at the same time support the right to have an abortion in situations where that power is lacking.[23] As we will see in the next chapter, some historical feminists advocated egregious violations of black women's reproductive autonomy. This has allowed the right to argue that those fighting for reproductive rights don't care about the black community, and that abortion can be slotted in the same category as coerced sterilization.

The same goes for the controversy around abortion and prenatal testing for disabilities like Down syndrome. Disabled people in our society face many difficulties. Families with disabled children get inadequate support. So upon learning that they might give birth to a disabled child, many people decide to have an abortion. Disabled people have also been the target of sterilization campaigns designed to limit childbirth. So it is understandable that prenatal testing might be problematic for those interested in disability justice. The right rarely advocates for supports that would help families raise disabled children or social changes that would make their lives easier. The mainstream reproductive rights movement generally doesn't either. Abortion rights supporters would benefit from a sustained disability justice perspective. Otherwise, for those who care about disabled people, the anti-abortion position can be easily presented as a better choice.

If right-wing organizations truly cared about social justice, equality, and saving lives, they would show it. They would spend more time advocating for universal childcare, support for single mothers, and other programs with positive effects on people's lives. They would spend less time trying to control people's sexuality and reproduction. Perhaps they would even advocate for paying for such social programs and supports by reducing spending on prisons and the military! It is easy to see how the weaknesses of the feminist movement have been translated into successful anti-abortion strategies. Feminist organizations working on reproductive issues, then, need to counter with a broader reproductive justice approach. This is both strategically important—and the right thing to do.

Another tactic of the religious right is to frame its coercive methods as service provision. Crisis Pregnancy Centres, or CPCs, are advertised as places you can go for help if you find yourself unintentionally pregnant. In general, they are designed to discourage women from having an abortion. They point to other options while spreading misinformation about abortion. NARAL Pro-Choice America (the former National Abortion and Reproductive Rights Action League) counts over 4,000 CPCs in the United States. As of 2008, Canadians for Choice counted 197 CPCs in Canada, most of them registered charities.[24] There are also CPCs in countries as diverse as Côte d'Ivoire, Ghana, Kenya, South Africa, Zambia, New Zealand, Namibia, Ireland, Mexico, and the Ukraine. Many are supported by larger organizations like Birthright International and Heartbeat International.

CPCs promote themselves as the caring wing of the religious right. Their advertising portrays them in an innocuous manner that disguises their political intentions. In the mid-size Canadian city of Kingston, Ontario, which has a population of about 117,000 and is home to a major university and two colleges, there are at least two Crisis Pregnancy Centres. Their "support services" are prominently advertised on city buses and sandwich boards. These ads claim the centres are supportive, non-judgmental, and confidential. If you are faced with an unintended pregnancy, you might think of CPCs as the place to go for help.

CPCs target younger women and people who don't know where to turn, especially if they are unable to seek the counsel of doctors or their families. The *Toronto Star* did an investigation in 2010 in the Greater Toronto Area. It found that CPCs presented themselves as providing information about all options, and downplayed the fact that they see abortion as always the wrong one.[25] Reporters were told that they increased their risk of breast cancer and fertility problems by having an abortion. But the U.S. National Cancer Institute, the Canadian Cancer Society, and the Society of Obstetricians and Gynaecologists of Canada have all concluded that no link between abortion and breast cancer exists. Likewise, the Royal College of Obstetricians and Gynaecologists in the United Kingdom has said that there is no proven link between abortions and infertility. As with any surgical procedure, there is some small risk of complications. The *Star* article cites data, though, suggesting that injury to the uterus occurs during less than one in 1,000 abortion procedures. The most comprehensive study of the safety of abortions to date, by researchers at the University of California San Francisco, suggests that major complications occur in only about one-quarter of one percent of procedures. By this measure, you could argue that giving birth is more dangerous than having an abortion.[26]

Many CPCs also provide counselling designed to promote the idea of "post-abortion syndrome." This condition is not recognized by the American Psychological Association. Preying on the stigma around abortion and the conflicted feelings that it may cause, CPCs encourage women to regret their abortions. Of course, abortions are not necessarily emotionally benign. Getting pregnant if you do not want a child or feel you are able to parent one is undeniably a stressful situation. So is making the decision to abort. Many people who have abortions do want children, but lack the needed economic resources or social supports. Complicated emotions around abortions, including feelings of regret, are entirely valid. But CPCs encourage people in a systematic and politicized way to regret their abortions. The hormonal drop-off that can occur with abortions (as well as with having carried a pregnancy to term) can cause depression. But it should be treated by trained counsellors and medical professionals, not religious organizations with a political agenda.

Frequently CPCs have a deceptive clinical atmosphere, designed to make people feel they are in a legitimate health care facility. Many are equipped with ultrasounds, which allow staff to present pictures of people's "babies." This tactic is designed to make them feel guilty about considering an abortion. Indeed, provoking feelings of guilt—over sexual behaviour, familial relationships, and thinking about abortion—is a way that CPCs manipulate people into other options. CPCs sometimes give out baby items. They may refer to abortion as "killing." And they may use developmentally incorrect fetal models to further make people feel ashamed of their decision.[27]

The growing sophistication of the anti-abortion movement's tactics is worrying. Its effect on the legal status of abortion has been variable, but it has ensured the persistence of stigma and attitudes that limit access to abortion. And it has served to highlight some weaknesses of the movement for reproductive rights, notably, the need for a sustained, holistic social justice perspective.

THE FIGHT FOR BETTER ACCESS

Where abortion is legal, the battleground shifts to ensuring widespread access. One approach to access is a service-oriented one. For example, it is often difficult to learn how and where to obtain abortions and referrals. So the National Abortion Federation in the United States operates a hotline to provide that information. There are similar hotlines in countries around the globe.

The Boston Women's Health Book Collective takes an educational approach. It helps people learn about their sexual and reproductive health and local political context. Since 1970, the collective has published research on women's health, giving women the tools to communicate with health care providers and challenge inadequate care. Its publication *Our Bodies, Ourselves* is now in its fifth edition. What began as a revolutionary pamphlet on sexuality and abortion has become the classic tome on women's health. Material from *Our Bodies, Ourselves* has been translated into thirty languages, adapted with local community organizations, and distributed globally.

Other approaches focus on overcoming barriers. The Abortion Support Network, a U.K.-based organization, helps people from Ireland and Northern Ireland travel to England to obtain an abortion. The network shares information about the closest and least costly places to get an abortion, and can sometimes provide accommodation or cover travel costs. Organizations across Europe—like Berlin-Irish Pro-choice Solidarity in Germany—help the network raise money with vibrant fundraising parties featuring music and performance art.

DIY Abortions

Self-induced or DIY abortions are not always unsafe. Criminalization makes them more dangerous. According to the Self Induced Abortion Legal Team—based out of Berkeley Law—most arrests for DIY abortions in the United States are made after seeking medical attention. So people with side effects may avoid seeking follow-up care. And people who unintentionally miscarry may be criminalized.

Abortions can be induced using herbs, pills, and other methods. There are various reasons to have an abortion outside a clinic or hospital. Lack of legal, affordable access to abortion services is a major one. Some people prefer traditional methods, others prefer the privacy of their own home, while others may simply believe in self-determining their health care. In some cases, having an abortion outside of the mainstream medical system is a form of resistance to Western, colonial health care.

No one deserves to be criminalized for accessing an abortion. Yet in the United States, up to forty laws could be broken in the course of a self-induced abortion. Because of racism and the over-policing of communities of colour, these laws come down especially hard on people of colour.

Source: "SIA Legal Team," Berkeley Law, www.law.berkeley.edu.

There is also a movement to support people in performing safe abortions themselves. While the drive to expand access to abortions by trained medical professionals continues, those who cannot access clinics or hospitals need support in accessing safe alternatives. There are also cultural, political, and personal reasons that someone might prefer to access an abortion outside of the medical system. Organizations like the Self Induced Abortion Legal Team in the United States and the international Women Help Women fight the criminalization of self-induced abortions. They train lay people to become safe providers and provide support for safely performing self-induced abortions.

There are efforts to expand access to the abortion pill, which makes medical rather than surgical abortions possible. The abortion pill—a combination of mifepristone and misoprostol—allows safe medical abortions early in pregnancy with less oversight from doctors. Misoprostol is available over the counter under different brand names in many countries—even in places where abortion is illegal. So people take it on its own to induce an abortion. It is considered safer and more effective to take abortion pills designed especially for that purpose. But these are more difficult to access in places where abortion is illegal. Organizations like Women on Web refer people to doctors who can ship them the abortion pill after an online consultation.

Inspired by the support birth doulas offer during labour and childbirth, abortion doulas perform a similar role for those needing abortions. They provide information and emotional support before, during, and after the procedure. The Sexual Health Resource Centre (SHRC) in Kingston offers abortion accompaniment services. Volunteers will go with a person seeking an abortion to as much of the appointment as they desire. This provides emotional support and meets hospital requirements to be accompanied home from a surgical abortion, which involves sedation. SHRC director Doulton Wiltshire says the service "allows for greater access, certainly, but it also allows you to keep your utilization of abortion services confidential—people have various reasons for not wanting to take friends or partners with them."

The SHRC spends one-fifth of its budget on bus ads, a direct response to those of the local CPCs. "The decision was made solely to ensure that if someone is unintentionally pregnant, and they see the Crisis Pregnancy Centre ad, they will also see our ad which states explicitly that we are pro-choice," Doulton told me. The bus ads have also allowed the SHRC to make a bigger impact. Doulton says they have seen a substantial increase in the number of community members using their services, indicating that these services are in demand.

The SHRC is located on a university campus. Support for abortion services has flourished on university campuses. But lately, there have been clashes between anti-abortion activists and other members of the campus community. Since students' views and beliefs are still being formed, schools are important sites for fighting stigma against abortion. Feminist organizations and women's centres often lead the charge. The year after the Genocide Awareness Project showed up at Saint Mary's University, the campus women's centre demonstrated the strength of alternative views. It produced Paula Kamen's play *Jane: Abortion and the Underground*, based on the story of the Chicago underground abortion service, and hosted a conference on reproductive justice. Other groups have hosted talks, initiated poster campaigns, or held counter-demos to those organized by anti-choice groups.

Progressive student unions also play a role. In Canada, student associations at several universities have banned anti-abortion groups from club status and support.[28] The Canadian Federation of Students has passed a resolution to support student unions that refuse to recognize anti-abortion clubs. There have been similar attempts, with varying success, at Oxford and Cardiff universities in the United Kingdom, Sydney University in Australia, and Biola University in the United States. These restrictions are often challenged on the basis of freedom of speech. But many unions have held to their belief that organizations promoting hateful or anti-woman views should not be validated. Anti-abortion groups are often financially supported by larger anti-abortion organizations, but these moves have helped to delegitimize their views on campuses.

High school students, too, have taken action. Organizations like NARAL Pro-Choice America have created programming to engage young people. The organization's Teen Outreach Reproductive Challenge combines peer reproductive health education with leadership opportunities. Students have also taken grass-roots initiatives. In 2011, a student at a Canadian Catholic high school was sent home for wearing a strip of tape on top of her uniform that said "pro-choice." Her action was in response to a similar school-sanctioned fundraising activity by pro-life students. Twenty-four other students joined in her protest. Canadian high school students have also protested the presence of the Canadian Centre for Bio-Ethical Reform near school property, blocking its graphic signs from the view of a nearby elementary school.

Little actions add up, and can lead to big changes. We've already touched on the fight for abortion access in Canada's east coast province of Prince Edward Island. In neighbouring New Brunswick, the recommendation of two doctors was until recently required before you could receive a funded hospital abortion. This practice had been abolished in most provinces since 1988. New Brunswick also required that abortions be performed by an obstetrician-gynecologist. And abortions accessed outside of hospitals were not covered by the provincial health care program.

The situation got worse when the Morgentaler clinic, operating without provincial support in the capital city of Fredericton, announced that it would shut its doors in 2014. Because it was difficult to access the procedure in hospitals, the clinic provided over 60 percent of abortions in the province.[29] Though the cost of an abortion at the clinic was high—ranging from C$700 to C$850—the clinic was vital. People reportedly began heading to the United States to seek services in private clinics,[30] using the abortion pill illegally, and otherwise attempting DIY abortions.

Long-running organizations—like the Abortion Rights Coalition of Canada and the National Abortion Federation—along with newer locally rooted organizations like Reproductive Justice New Brunswick and the Young Feminists youth group demanded access to fully funded abortions. Meanwhile, Maritime Abortion Support Services offered support to anyone in New Brunswick needing to travel to undergo the procedure. It set up billeting, provided transportation, and arranged informal informational meetings with people who had had abortions.

The lack of access to abortion became an issue in the province's elections, and Brian Gallant, the newly elected premier, announced that a regulation removing the two-doctor requirement would come into effect on January 1, 2015. It puts abortion in the same category as other medical procedures covered by provincial health insurance. Shortly thereafter, Prince Edward Island announced that it would begin providing Island women with local access to abortion by 2017.

It remains to be seen how these policy changes will affect access to abortions on the ground. And when you consider the breadth of approaches that would effectively give people control over their reproductive lives, abortion access is only the tip of the iceberg. But nonetheless, these were huge victories for people in the region. They demonstrate the wins that grassroots pressure can achieve.

4

THE
HISTORY OF
COERCIVE
STERILIZATION

FIRST HEARD the term "eugenics" in the context of the Holocaust. Nazi Germany's obsession with creating a "superior" Aryan race was inspired by this ideology. Eugenics promoted the improvement of the human breeding stock. It discouraged reproduction among people who were considered undesirable. This ideology was another way that the state justified control over reproduction to serve political and economic goals.

When I learned about eugenics in high school, my teachers never mentioned how pervasive these ideas were. Maybe they didn't know. The Nazis' horrific attempt to eradicate Jewish, disabled, and queer people through concentration camps and forcible sterilization was well known. But eugenics laws were also enacted in countries as diverse as the United States, Canada, India, Sweden, and Japan. In fact, the state of California sterilized over 20,000 people from 1909 to 1963, and it was California's eugenically motivated sterilization laws that inspired Germany's.[1]

Eugenics programs and sterilization campaigns were formalized into law in many countries and were seriously debated in many more. Other sterilization campaigns occurred outside of any formal legislation. Many of the programs focused on people with disabilities. But who met this definition was strongly related to race, poverty, and in women, higher levels of sexual activity. Inevitably, eugenics legislation served political goals of population control. In Canada and the United States, Indigenous women were disproportionately targeted for sterilization. There, eugenics programs supported a colonial project to clear the land of Indigenous peoples. In the United States, black women were among those most likely to be sterilized without consent. This effort to control the size of the black population was a manifestation of white supremacy.

Some programs had procedures to obtain consent from the people who were to be sterilized. But these procedures were often questionable. In other regions, there was no such requirement. For example, when the eugenics law in the Canadian province of Alberta was modified in 1935, the requirement to obtain consent was removed for anyone deemed "mentally defective." In some cases, people were sterilized not just without their consent, but also without their knowledge.

After learning about this shocking history, I wondered why I had not been taught it in school. Maybe it's easier to pretend these things don't happen so close to home. My teachers spent plenty of class time criticizing women who chose to have abortions. They should have also found time to condemn governments that sterilized people without their consent. The control that religions and governments exercise over reproduction has never really been about saving the unborn. It's about maintaining relations of power. The power of governments over populations, of men over women, of settlers over Indigenous people, and of white people over people of colour.

This is as true now as it was in the past. And the history is not all that ancient. Most places abolished their eugenics programs after the horrors of the Holocaust were brought to light. But formal eugenics legislation lasted in some places until the early 1970s. And although eugenics laws have largely been abolished, similar policies and practices continue today. Coercive sterilizations, though they are typically illegal, still happen in Europe and North

Reproduction and Migration

States control population by enforcing borders and controlling who can access citizenship. Most modern states were established through colonization and are maintained through similarly violent and exclusionary policies. Well-known migrant justice activist Harsha Walia calls this "border imperialism." People with financial resources or professional credentials can cross borders easily; people from lower classes are kept out. This is a form of social control, and it protects economic interests. Preventing people from moving to places with better wages and conditions upholds the very low wages paid in some parts of the Global South. People who do make it across borders are marginalized so that they can be easily exploited as workers.

A poignant connection between migration and reproduction is foreign domestic workers. Women, lacking sufficient employment in their own countries, are brought in as nannies to care for Canadian and American families. They must leave their own children behind, and often lack the benefits of citizenship in their new home. In Canada, domestic workers must have full-time work for two years before they can apply for permanent residency and to bring their children over. In the United States, foreign domestic workers rely on an employer's sponsorship while applying for a green card, a process that takes a couple of years. Domestic workers are unable to parent their own children, and their reliance on employers to access immigration channels make them vulnerable to abuse.

Sources: Rhacel Salazar Parennas, *The Force of Domesticity: Filipina Migrants and Globalization* (New York: New York University Press, 2008); Harsha Walia, *Undoing Border Imperialism* (Oakland: AK Press, 2013).

America. Between 2006 and 2010, at least 148 women at a prison in California were sterilized at government expense without their consent.[2] And in the Global South, sterilizations continue as population control measures.

Interestingly, in the years before abortion and birth control were decriminalized, middle-class women who wanted to be sterilized to avoid pregnancy were often denied. This is a stark example of the interaction of justice, access, and consent. Sterilizations were reserved for those considered undesirable, whether they wanted them or not. Desirable people were encouraged to have children, whether they wanted them or not. Both practices manipulated who would give birth to the next generation of citizens, in the service of economic and political interests.

A SHORT HISTORY OF EUGENICS IDEAS

Eugenics is usually traced to British scientist Francis Galton. Galton, a relative of Charles Darwin, was interested in applying Darwin's theories of natural selection to humans. Galton pursued mathematical and biological studies to look for a hereditary basis for "desirable" human characteristics. In 1883, Galton coined the term "eugenics" to mean "nobility in birth." Universities throughout Europe and the United States quickly began to investigate the subject.

This occurred at a time when British society was rapidly changing. The onset of capitalism brought with it industrialization and social upheaval. The Industrial Revolution created an increase in productivity. But as more people moved into the cities looking for work, the population of the urban poor exploded. Factory owners lived comfortably, and a middle class of professionals emerged. General workers, meanwhile, faced malnutrition, poor working conditions, dilapidated housing, and disease.

The middle and upper classes were eager to prevent revolutionary activity among the new urban poor. For solutions, they looked to the scientists' research on heredity. Elites were benefiting from capitalist industrialization. So they didn't typically recognize poverty as a social issue caused by increasing inequality. Instead, they believed that people who were poor were inherently inferior. This position fit neatly with eugenics research into the hereditability of social characteristics.

Scientifically questionable findings linked poverty and criminal behaviour with biology. Wealthy reformers thought that by limiting the prevalence of certain genes within a population, they could limit undesirable social characteristics. In Britain, this usually referred to poverty. But in other places, particularly the United States, undesirable genetic traits were strongly linked to race. The claim of genetic differences among races became a powerful way to justify white supremacy. Eugenics evolved from the study of heredity to a politicized project. It sought to eliminate undesirable traits from the population by controlling reproduction. Those with undesirable traits would be unable to pass their genes along to their children.

These were not fringe ideas. Eugenics-based thinking became popular across the political spectrum. The idea of the state planning the characteristics of its citizenry became popular even among socialists who were committed to utopian ideals. Many prominent thinkers supported the eugenics movement. The list includes inventor Alexander Graham Bell, playwright Bernard Shaw, and British prime minister Winston Churchill.

EUGENICS IN PRACTICE

The idea of eugenics was birthed in the United Kingdom. It was first translated into practice in the United States. After slavery was abolished, U.S. society was fraught with racial tensions. Many wealthy white Americans were attracted to the manipulation of heredity. They wanted to create a society made up of people just like them.[3] In 1907, the state of Indiana enacted the world's first eugenically motivated sterilization law. The law allowed for the involuntary sterilization of "confirmed criminals, idiots, imbeciles, and rapists." Eugenics also took hold in California, where immigration had shifted the characteristics of the population.

A compulsory sterilization law similar to Indiana's was introduced in 1909. California became a hotbed for eugenics activity. Its high rate of sterilization and fervent promotion of the practice were an inspiration for Adolf Hitler.

Eugenics campaigns quickly spread across the country. Thirty U.S. states had formal eugenics legislation. Due to poorly kept records and under-the-radar procedures, we will never know exactly how many people suffered. But estimates suggest that approximately 60,000 people were sterilized in state-sanctioned procedures.[4] And this may be a conservative number. California alone sterilized a whopping 9,782 people, mostly women, in the first twenty-five years of its eugenics legislation.[5]

In Canada, sterilization laws came into effect in Alberta in 1928 and in British Columbia in 1933. These laws were rescinded in the 1970s. By then, 2,822 people in Alberta and about 200 in British Columbia had been sterilized, often without their consent. In Ontario, it is estimated that over 1,000 people were sterilized, 580 of whom were Indigenous.[6] Alberta had a particular enthusiasm for eugenics activity. The Alberta legislation was passed after years of campaigning by prominent social reformers. They believed that immigrants of inferior genetic stock were to blame for crime, sex work, and unemployment. These characteristics were linked to being "feebleminded."

By 1940, eugenics had spread across Europe. It was practised in countries including Sweden, Denmark, Estonia, Finland, Iceland, and Norway. Denmark was one of the first to enact sterilization legislation in the 1930s. Eleven thousand people were sterilized while the law was in effect. In Norway, approximately 44,000 people were sterilized between 1934 and 1977. Sweden sterilized an estimated 63,000 people. It was the country with the second-highest rate of sterilizations, second only to Nazi Germany.[7]

Eugenics policies took different shapes in different countries. In general, though, sterilization campaigns aimed to ensure a particular kind of population. They typically favoured citizens who were white, wealthy, and able-bodied. People with disabilities were targeted, in part, because mental disabilities supposedly had a biological basis. But the notion of "disability" is constructed. Social relations set standards for bodies and marginalize those who don't conform. In this sense, eugenics thinking helped reinforce the idea of disability, as it did the idea of race.

Laws allowed sterilization of the "feebleminded," the "unfit," and the "mentally defective." People were targeted based on their performance on intelligence tests, or for a diagnosis of psychosis, neurosyphilis, epilepsy, or Huntington's chorea. In Alberta, the Sexual Sterilization Act stated that those in mental health institutions were candidates for sterilization if they might be eligible for discharge once the risk of "evil by transmission of the disability" was removed. Yes, you read that right. People with disabilities were seen as doing evil by daring to have babies. This was a clear affront to their sexual and reproductive freedoms.

Not just anyone met these definitions. Their application was strongly related to race, class, and other characteristics of an "ideal citizen." In fact, how capable a parent someone was considered to be was often just as important a criterion for sterilization as biological heritability. In some U.S. states, programs targeted people with physical disabilities, alcoholism, or criminal records, people receiving state assistance, orphans, and even victims of rape. In Sweden, the 1934 Sterilization Act allowed sterilization for medical reasons, to prevent people with disabilities from passing on their genes. It also allowed sterilization for social reasons—even if it was recognized that the social problem had no genetic basis. There are reports of schoolchildren being sterilized if they failed to keep up. People facing chronic poverty, alcoholism, or homelessness were sterilized. One young woman in Sweden was targeted when she fell behind in school. Doctors claimed she came from a family with a history of alcoholism, promiscuity, and mental illness. It turned out her poor academic showing was because she had poor vision. She needed glasses, but got her ovaries removed.[8]

These campaigns often targeted people considered to be of loose moral character. They were used to regulate—and punish—

Disability Justice and Reproductive Justice

People with disabilities are often stereotyped as childlike and helpless—and asexual. They aren't always offered health services like Pap smears or birth control. Society also casts disabled women as incapable mothers, so they have difficulty adopting. Yet with supports and adaptations, they are often perfectly capable parents. Cribs can be lowered to the height of a wheelchair; alarms can trigger lights when a child cries. Disability activists have shown that who is capable of parenting has more to do with the ways our society is set up than with individual abilities. But modifications don't come cheap, and disabled women often have lower incomes. If a disabled woman needs help, she may have to contact social services. This subjects her to surveillance and the risk of her children being taken away.

The disability justice community has contributed to how we think about access. Health care and other systems are set up to best support young, white, able-bodied, economically privileged, straight men in urban centres. Anyone who deviates from this "norm"—many of us—faces additional barriers.

Disability justice also stresses community access, in which people share resources and capacities to collectively meet each other's needs. In such a community, people can be self-sufficient but also get much-needed support, for example, mutual aid in parenting. Few parents have access to all the support they need. So the movement around reproductive issues can learn much from disability justice approaches.

Sources: Mia Mingus, "Disabled Women and Reproductive Justice," Pro-Choice Public Education Project, http://protectchoice.org; "The Only Parent in the Neighborhood: Mothering and Women with Disabilities," DAWN-RAFH Canada, www.dawncanada.net; Jewelles Smith, "Disabled Mothering: Building a Safe and Accessible Community," DAWN-RAFH Canada.

female sexuality. This was especially the case after the Second World War, when increases in divorce and premarital sex were seen as threats to a country's moral standing. Some people were targeted because they were patients at psychiatric institutions or it was recommended by a teacher. Others were labelled mentally deficient after being picked up by police for sex work.[9] In Sweden, where approximately 90 percent of those sterilized were women,[10] some women seeking abortions were also forced to consent to sterilization as a condition. Religion was invoked to prevent voluntary access to contraceptives, abortion, and elective sterilization. At the same time, eugenically motivated sterilization campaigns sought to enforce morality and create "God's plan for a perfect community."[11]

The criteria of race and ethnicity were tied to colonial and white supremacist goals. To enforce their vision of a desirable society, many eugenicists supported stricter immigration laws. Sterilization campaigns, too, disproportionately affected people of colour and ethnic groups. Their racial bias was stark in the United States. North Carolina adopted sterilization campaigns with particular enthusiasm. In that state, 65 percent of sterilization procedures were performed on black women. By the 1970s, almost one-quarter of Indigenous women between the ages of 15 and 44 in the United States had been sterilized.[12]

The criteria to recommend people for sterilization did not necessarily name race. But in societies marked by deep racial inequality, people who met the criteria were often people of colour. For example, immigrants and people with less formal education would likely score low on IQ tests. They might be deemed feeble-minded on that basis, though IQ tests are now recognized as a culturally specific and subjective measure of intelligence. Because of systemic racism, people of colour were more likely to live in poverty and receive state assistance. Likewise, inmates of prisons or mental health institutions were targets of sterilization campaigns. Even today, people of colour and Indigenous people are overrepresented in U.S. and Canadian prisons. It is easy to see how people of colour were the de facto targets of these campaigns—especially if they were also poor or also had disabilities.

In Sweden and other Nordic countries, on the other hand, sterilization campaigns were explicitly used for ethnic cleansing. The Roma people were particularly targeted. Grounds for recommending sterilization included "unmistakable Gypsy features, psychopathy, [and] vagabond life."[13] Coercive sterilization was one way to eradicate the Roma population within Swedish borders. The movement of the traditionally nomadic people was also limited. And "race inventories" were used by the State Institute for Racial Biology at Uppsala University to control the Roma and keep them from accessing civil rights.[14] There is also evidence that the Saami people—the Indigenous population ancestral to Swedish territory, who faced segregation and assimilation—were targeted for sterilization.[15]

In Canada, Indigenous people were disproportionately targeted for sterilization. Colonial history has resulted in many Indigenous people living in poverty. It has also perpetuated a stereotype of deviant sexuality. Both of these conditions would attract the attention of eugenicists. With this in mind, it isn't surprising that many Indigenous people would be labelled "mentally defective." Eugenics was also a civilizing mission of sorts. In line with broader colonial policy, eugenicists believed it would be best for Indigenous people for their populations to decline. This policy ultimately supported the cultural and racial destruction of Indigenous people.

In Ontario, the federal government may have paid for sterilizations through Indian Health Services. In 1937, the Department of Indian Affairs in Alberta suggested that consent for sterilizations be obtained whenever possible. It wanted to avoid accusations that sterilization constituted "a conspiracy for the elimination of the race." When the law was changed later that year so that consent was no longer required, sterilizations of Indigenous people rose sharply. They tripled from 1949 to 1959.[16]

There is also evidence that Indigenous people were targeted in Canada's North. In 1973 the Canadian Broadcasting Corporation reported that there was a calculated attempt to reduce the birth rate among the Inuit. Inuit children sent away for medical treatment were never returned to their families, and Inuit women were sterilized without their consent. The government vigorously denied these claims. But in this same period, an estimated 3,406 Indigenous people were forcibly sterilized without consent in the United States, so the accusations seem plausible.[17] Ultimately a Canadian parliamentary inquiry confirmed that seventy steriliza- tions had been carried out between 1966 and 1976. It is not known how many were involuntary. And the inquiry may have ignored areas that were known to have higher rates of sterilization.[18]

At the height of the Great Depression, poor and working-class people were often targeted. Wealthy business owners saw large populations of the working poor as a threat to their power. Cana- dian businessman A.R. Kaufman is often praised for making con- traception information available to less privileged communities. But he also led the charge for eugenics activity in Ontario. Kaufman encouraged his factory workers to get sterilized at his expense. At a time of high unemployment, few of them were in a position to argue with their boss.[19] As president of the Kaufman Rubber Com- pany in Kitchener, Kaufman was a vocal opponent of unions and organized labour. He believed that by limiting the population of the poor, he would also limit revolutionary activity. A member of the Eugenics Society of Canada, Kaufman was instrumental in encouraging doctors in Ontario to perform sterilizations on impoverished people. The province had no sterilization law. And in an era in which contraception and abortion were still criminalized, many doctors would likely have been reluctant to perform them.

Together with everyday racism and prejudice, these strong political motives allowed sterilization campaigns to persist for as long as they did. In the face of mounting resistance, the laws were ultimately challenged. In Los Angeles, ten Mexican women suc- cessfully sued the hospital where they had been sterilized without consent. In New York, the Committee to End Sterilization Abuse drafted guidelines to prevent non-consensual sterilizations. The

Committee to End Sterilization Abuse

The Committee to End Sterilization Abuse (CESA) was formed in New York. This group of women was committed to ending non-consensual and coercive sterilization practices aimed at disadvantaged women. The committee was instrumental in creating guidelines for sterilization practices in New York City. In 1979 it played a pivotal role in passing national sterilization guidelines. CESA was often met with hostility from the rest of the women's movement, which included white women who wanted to access sterilization themselves.

A prominent member of CESA was Dr. Helen Rodriguez-Trias, a pediatrician of Puerto Rican descent. She saw first-hand the impact of racism, restrictive abortion laws, and coercive sterilization practices on disadvantaged communities. Rodriguez-Trias became a tireless advocate for women's health for all women, not just the privileged middle class.

Coercive sterilization has been formally abolished in the United States. But Rodriguez-Trias maintains that not-so-subtle coercion continues as a result of inadequate abortion services, lack of health insurance, and welfare reform that discourages low-income people from having kids.

Source: Joyce Wilcox, "The Face of Women's Health: Helen Rodriguez-Trias," *American Journal of Public Health* 92,4 (2002), 566–9.

guidelines included waiting periods before the surgery and full access to a range of contraception options.

Most sterilization legislation was repealed by the early 1980s. Some U.S. states—including North Carolina and Virginia—have apologized for the abuses of this period. North Carolina has introduced a compensation program. To date the U.S. federal government has not apologized. And periodic reports continue to surface of vulnerable people being sterilized without consent.

Alberta's sterilization law was revoked in 1972 on the grounds that it violated human rights. Faced with court cases and mounting pressure from survivors, the Alberta government issued an apology in 1999. In British Colombia, sterilization legislation was revoked in 1973. But advocacy groups suggest that the practice continued until the Supreme Court ruled in 1986 that sterilization should not be permitted without consent.[20] In Sweden, eugenics policies came to an end in 1975. But mandatory sterilization for people wishing to change their gender persisted until 2012. And even where apologies have been issued, governments still pursue policies that further colonial, racist, and ableist objectives. People who live with poverty, Indigenous people, people of colour, and disabled people continue to face threats to autonomy over their reproductive lives.

EUGENICS AND FEMINISM

When I was learning about these issues, I was shocked at the way these draconian campaigns coexisted with social justice ideas. I was particularly surprised to learn of the history of eugenics campaigns in places like Sweden and Denmark. These Nordic countries are often praised by progressives. They have peaceful foreign policy, comprehensive health and education systems, and strong social safety nets. Yet these admirable policies coexisted with egregious human rights abuses. This is another reminder of the need for social justice for all, not just the privileged few.

Work on reproductive issues—and feminism in general—has its own shady history. First-wave feminists and early women's rights campaigners were vocal supporters of eugenics campaigns. While fighting for rights and justice for some, many early feminists campaigned to take away the rights of others.

Perhaps you have heard of Victoria Woodhull, the first woman to run for president of the United States. You may know that she was the first woman to address a congressional committee, the first to run a brokerage firm on Wall Street, and one of the first to start a newspaper. She was a political radical, who published the first English translation of Karl Marx's *Communist Manifesto*. And she advocated for the right of women to vote and divorce. But you likely haven't heard that Woodhull, despite believing in "free love" without government interference, also believed that "the overworked, the badly bred, and the overfed" should not be allowed to have children.[21] Some even consider her—rather than Francis Galton—the pioneering force behind the spread of eugenics ideas.[22]

Perhaps you have heard of the Famous Five—who advocated for women to be considered "persons" under Canadian law. If you went to high school in Canada, that may well the extent of feminist or social movement history that was covered. These women were determined activists who started a petition to have the issue considered in court, and gained women the right to representation in the Senate. But Emily Murphy, one of the Famous Five, also wrote a book called *The Black Candle*. It described an international conspiracy of non-whites to contaminate the white race using drugs. Murphy also actively advocated for the deportation of immigrants. A 2012 article in *Maclean's* magazine called her a "xenophobic fascist." She also claimed that the feebleminded were not entitled to have offspring. Nellie McClung, perhaps the most famous of the five, was a fervent advocate of Alberta's eugenics law. In fact, the Famous Five were part of the women's wing of the United Farmers of Alberta—the group that first discussed and drafted the province's Sexual Sterilization Act.

The strange mix of racism, ableism, and feminism advanced by the Famous Five was, unfortunately, not so strange at the time. Women's rights were often promoted along with "good morals" and the purity of the white race. Margaret Sanger was the founder of Planned Parenthood, perhaps the most well known sexual and reproductive health organization today. She was also a well-known eugenicist. Sanger believed that contraception was the only practical way to prevent unsafe illegal abortions. She contributed to the struggle for accessible birth control, but she also believed in reducing the populations of the "unfit." Sanger advocated family planning initiatives, strict immigration controls, and compulsory sterilization for those deemed mentally inferior. Her fervent activism for birth control stemmed largely from her eugenics beliefs.

Likewise, Marie Stopes was a well-known advocate of birth control in Britain. Her legacy lives on through the Marie Stopes International organization. Stopes was also a prominent eugenicist who advocated for the sterilization of the unfit, and who corresponded with Adolf Hitler. She famously wrote her son out of her will when he married a woman with an eye condition. "By marrying her," she claimed, "he had betrayed his parents and made a mock of [their] life's work for breeding and the race."[23]

This history is shameful. But it is also part of the history of feminism and of reproductive rights. It shows us where the historical feminist movement came up short. By caring only for some women, it helped perpetuate gross injustices. Knowing these stories, we can see where fractures in the contemporary struggle for reproductive rights come from. It isn't surprising that women who had historically been targeted for sterilization might distrust fights for greater abortion access.

These stories also reinforce how important it is to think about reproductive issues holistically. They are issues not just of women's rights but also of broader justice. In accessing and consenting to reproductive options, women from different backgrounds have different needs and different barriers. And an individual's reproductive choices should never be controlled for social, economic, or political purposes.

STERILIZATION AND CONSENT

At the heart of resistance to sterilization campaigns is the issue of consent. People should be able to decide for themselves whether to be sterilized or not. They should have access to all the information about the procedure, and other options for avoiding or terminating pregnancies should be easily accessible.

The Case of Leilani Muir

The scrapping of sterilization laws, the compensation offered to those who were sterilized, and government apologies have only come about because of the resistance and determination of the people involved. Leilani Muir, who was sterilized in Alberta, underwent the procedure at the age of fourteen. She was told she was having her appendix removed. Because she filed a successful lawsuit against the provincial government, her story is one of the few well-known cases of resistance to the eugenics law in Canada.

Muir lived in a poor and abusive family in rural Alberta, until she was dropped off at the Provincial Training School for Mental Defectives with little known justification other than being unwanted by her mother. She was presented to the Eugenics Board after scoring low on an IQ test, and recommended for sterilization. She did not know that she had been sterilized until years later, when, having been released from the institution, she married and tried to have kids.

While other survivors of the sterilization law settled their cases out of court, Muir pursued legal action to draw attention to the injustices she and countless others suffered. This case raised awareness of the history of forced sterilization in Canada. The Alberta government was forced to apologize for the campaign and awarded damages to the people affected. Muir's story is the subject of a 1996 National Film Board of Canada documentary, *The Sterilization of Leilani Muir*.

Eugenically motivated sterilization campaigns do not make true consent possible. Some people who were targeted by eugenics campaigns may have genuinely wanted to be sterilized anyway. Some privileged people did, so this isn't an unreasonable assumption. But eugenics campaigns made sterilization dehumanizing and demeaning. As they targeted only certain groups of people for sterilization, the possibility of their consent was limited from the outset.

As the laws evolved, the limited nature of consent was often made clear. In Alberta, in the early years of the sterilization laws, the consent of the person or their family was required before the procedure could take place. Predictably, this consent was difficult to obtain. So the government decided that rather than let people make decisions for themselves, it would instead remove the formal requirement of consent.

Even where consent was required, in practice it was far from free and fully informed consent. Misinformation has often been used to convince people to "consent" to sterilization. It was disturbingly common for people to be told—even without legal basis—that their immigration status would be at risk if they were not sterilized. Or that their government benefits would be withheld, or that their children would be taken from them.[24] In other cases, people have been tricked into having the procedure. In the southern United States, involuntary, non-consensual sterilization was so recognized that it earned a nickname: the Mississippi appendectomy. The term was coined by civil rights leader Fannie Lou Hamer. Women of colour would go to their doctors with unrelated medical conditions and end up sterilized. They would have unrelated operations and end up sterilized. Or they would be told they were having appendectomies but would—you guessed it!—end up sterilized.

I've already mentioned how difficult it would be to refuse sterilization if your boss requested it at a time when jobs are scarce. People lacked the ability to choose in many other ways too. In Alberta, when consent was still formally required, people were told that they had to consent to the sterilization in order to be released from an institution. In at least a few cases, they were incarcerated if they refused. Some people consented to the procedure but were told it was temporary—akin to a contraceptive technique.

In Puerto Rico, the U.S. government initiated a campaign in 1936 to encourage Puerto Rican women to get sterilized. Sterilizations were technically voluntary, but they were so heavily pushed on women that their ability to truly consent was limited. Government officials and health workers—backed by funding from the U.S. government—went door to door to promote the procedure. Sometimes being sterilized was presented as a requirement for employment. Sterilization—which was offered for free—was sometimes seen as the only option at a time when other methods of contraception were not available. Often women would undergo the procedure thinking it was reversible. By 1965 one-third of Puerto Rican mothers aged 20 to 49 had been sterilized—a rate 10 times that of U.S. women generally.[25] Women's organizations have raised the injustices of the sterilization campaign as part of calling for the territory's independence.

Another factor that limits true consent to sterilization has been the unavailability of contraception or abortion. Someone might have no other option to limit family size. This would have been common during the time that eugenics campaigns were most active. If people faced crippling poverty without adequate social supports, it is not so surprising that they might agree to sterilization. Upper- and middle-class white women, who faced fewer social and economic barriers, sought sterilizations to limit family size. Many had to pursue them secretly, though. Even today, in the absence of formal eugenics programs, scholar Andrea Smith has spoken of the danger of "restrictive abortion policies combined with lenient sterilization policies" in Indigenous communities.[26] This combination leads to higher rates of sterilization, with genocidal implications.

All of this is to say that sterilization itself is not a problem. It is the lack of consent that makes eugenically motivated sterilization unsavoury. Today, people of all genders seek and consent to surgical sterilization as a form of birth control. Historically, middle-class women sought sterilizations in resistance to oppressive abortion and contraceptive laws. But even today, in the absence of formal sterilization laws, some people are encouraged and others are discouraged from accessing sterilization. I know of several young, white, middle-class women who have asked their doctor about sterilization but have been refused the procedure. Usually they are told that they are too young and might regret it later. But those who are seen as less desirable parents are treated much differently. U.S.-based Project Prevention offers women addicted to drugs US$300 to get sterilized. While some addicts may genuinely want to be sterilized, it is reasonable to assume that many will resort to it out of desperation. This is not true consent. Even without formal eugenics programs, the ability to consent to sterilization is still strongly shaped by who is considered worthy or unworthy to parent and have children.

5

COERCIVE STERILIZATION TODAY

EUGENICS has long fallen out of favour. The horrific human rights abuses of these campaigns are now widely recognized. But unfortunately, politics continues to shape who retains their ability to have children. Some people globally still struggle to access safe abortions. At the same time, others are concerned with protecting their ability to have children.

From 1978 to 2015, China's infamous one-child policy limited most Chinese couples in urban areas to just one child. (In 2016, the law was changed to permit two children.) In addition to forcing abortion on many couples, this policy resulted in high rates of female infanticide. In a country where men are seen as more valuable, the female birth rate declined.

This is just one well-known case. In many European countries, trans people are forced to submit to sterilization as a condition of changing their legal gender. In much of the Global South, sterilization is a common method of population control. The use of long-acting contraceptives with dangerous side effects has also emerged as a way to control the fertility of vulnerable women. Explicit eugenics laws may be dead. But we are haunted by a legacy that considers some people's reproductive capacities expendable for political goals.

TRANS COMMUNITIES
AND STERILIZATION

In 2012, Sweden made global headlines for contemporary policies of forced sterilization. If people wanted to legally change their
gender, they were forced to submit to sterilization first. According
to the Swedish Federation for Lesbian, Gay, Bisexual and Transgender Rights, approximately five hundred trans people were sterilized under coercion in Sweden between 1972 and 2012. The issue
gained attention that year after an unsuccessful attempt to repeal
the law. Given Sweden's reputation for being "gay-friendly" and
progressive, many found the Swedish case shocking. But its policy was not that unusual. In 2013, Transgender Europe found that
twenty-four European countries required sterilization to legally
change gender. Among them were Italy, France, Belgium, and
Norway.[1]

The rationale for these laws is that individuals need to "prove"
they are serious about wanting to change gender. So serious medical intervention—gender reassignment surgery and sexual sterilization—is required. This is a heteropatriarchal perspective.
It narrowly equates gender, which is socially and culturally constructed, with biological sex and reproductive capacities. These
laws reinforce static categories of what it means to be a man and
a woman. They deny the possibility of any in-between or other
space. For example, they prevent the cultural challenge posed by a
trans man becoming pregnant. More importantly, these laws deny
individual trans people the right to self-determine what changing
gender looks like for them.

Of course, under these laws, trans people could "choose" not
to legally change their gender. That would avoid the necessity
of sterilization. But when the gender on your legal documents is
different from your gender identity, that comes with its own set of
challenges. Practically, it means that a trans person would have to
explain themselves every time they needed to present identifica-
tion. Having to explain the difference between the gender on their

documents and their gender presentation would at best be uncomfortable and emotional trying. At worst, it could prevent someone from crossing a border, opening a bank account, or finding employment. Identity documents that match the gender with which a person identifies can help them feel comfortable and respected in their gender identity. For many trans and gender non-conforming people, changing legal gender is an important matter.

Which brings us, again, to the matter of consent. Technically these sterilization procedures are consensual. Anecdotes suggest that the process for obtaining formal consent is extremely thorough.[2] But these laws put trans people in an impossible situation in which true consent is virtually impossible. You may be fully informed about the procedure and sign your name on the dotted line. But if the other available options are so painful or difficult that you feel you have no choice but to agree, then consent is meaningless. Trans people who want to be sterilized should be able to do so. But it should not come as a requirement for legally changing gender.

Organizations like Transgender Europe have brought worldwide attention to this issue. The World Health Organization has affirmed that "transgender and intersex persons should be able to access health services, including contraceptive services such as sterilization, on the same basis as others: free from coercion, discrimination, and violence."[3] Action on the issue has led to real changes for trans people. Sweden did change its law to allow gender changes independent of reproductive capacities. Other countries have followed suit. Denmark's laws became among the most progressive. Now, trans people in Denmark do not have to be sterilized to change their gender identities. They also don't have to submit to other commonly required psychological or medical procedures. Instead, they only have to fill out some paperwork. This policy is an important step forward in trans people's ability to self-determine their gender identity.

For many trans people across Europe, though, the threat of coercive sterilization continues. Such laws are a disturbing reminder that the right to bear children or to simply have bodily integrity and self-determination remains under threat. This is especially the case for people who are already misunderstood or marginalized.

POPULATION CONTROL AND STERILIZATION

In international development circles, population control has now replaced eugenics as a buzzword. But many of its impacts are similar. Global organizations still try to control the birth rate of particular groups of women. Typically, the poorest. Population control programs are often couched in the language of women's rights. But they focus on reducing populations, not on women's empowerment. In fact, it was because of this tension that women of colour originally adopted a reproductive justice framework.

Population control efforts draw inspiration from the writings of Thomas Malthus. During the Industrial Revolution in Britain, Malthus predicted that the global population would grow at a faster rate than global resources, particularly food. He blamed the suffering in society on population growth, not on the upheaval caused by the transition to capitalism. He suggested that poverty, famine, and war were necessary evils that kept population growth under control. In particular, Malthus advocated for the removal of the Poor Laws that provided some state support for the poorest people.

Malthus's predictions were wrong. He didn't take into account advances in agricultural production rates, and he discounted the role of human decision-making in limiting population growth. But Malthusian ideas continue to be influential. In 1968, Paul Ehrlich wrote *The Population Bomb*. This book, too, warned of the dangers of overpopulation. It gave particular attention to out-of-control population growth in the Global South. Fuelling fears that the non-white population would swamp the Global North, Ehrlich argued for cutting off food aid to those countries considered beyond redemption. The book explicitly raised the possibility of using reproductive technologies to limit population growth. It even floated, and then rejected, the idea of adding sterilizing agents to the water supply.

Population control is now used to justify sterilization of poor people in the Global South. As in the case of China, some campaigns come at the behest of national governments that fear the crunch of overpopulation. In India in 1975, Indian Prime Minister Indira Gandhi declared a draconian Emergency Period to deal with social unrest. Among a litany of human rights abuses, the government used bribes and other coercive measures to sterilize 8.3 million poor women and men. The stage had been set for this initiative by international support for "modernizing" India, including the promotion of birth control.

Today India continues to use involuntary sterilization as a population control measure. Horror stories abound. In 2013 reports surfaced of a mass sterilization procedure. A hundred women were afterwards dragged out into a field to recover.[4] In 2014, eleven women died in a similar government-run sterilization camp.[5] Other stories have emerged of botched operations. Women are left to bleed. Pregnant women are sterilized, resulting in miscarriages.[6] The international community bears some responsibility. The U.K. government knew that sterilization was the most commonly advocated form of birth control in India. But in 2012, it still funded India's "reproductive health" program to a tune of £166 million.

Often population control campaigns have clear political motivations. During the colonial period, for example, British officials focused on high fertility rates in India. Burgeoning native populations, they feared, would be harder to control. During the Cold War, the United States focused on population as a security concern. Young, growing populations in the Global South would be more likely to resist transnational corporations or advocate for better distribution of wealth. During this time, the U.S. government helped establish the United Nations Fund for Population

Activities (now the UN Population Fund) and set up federal funding for foreign population control.

Within national borders, immigrants or other people who are deemed undesirable are the most likely to be involuntary sterilized.[7] Coercive sterilization of the Roma population is still common in the Czech Republic, Hungary, and Slovakia.[8] HIV-positive women in Namibia are routinely sterilized without giving consent.[9] Similar cases have been reported in South Africa.[10] Mexico is lauded for its declining birth rates. But poor women there have been sterilized during unnecessary Caesarean sections. In Uzbekistan, some low-income women were asked for a certificate of sterilization as a condition of employment.[11] Everywhere, it's people who lack social, political, and economic power who are most at risk.

The UN Population Fund, the World Bank, and various foreign aid agencies help set national targets for population control. The targets are often worked into Structural Adjustment Programs. The U.S. foreign aid agency, USAID, has funded family planning initiatives that aim to meet drastic population reduction targets. This can have disastrous results for women. For example, in 1996 USAID funded a population program in Peru. Over a five-year period, it aimed to reduce the number of births from 3.2 births to 2.5 births per woman. Under a right-wing government known for human rights violations, Peru initiated sterilization programs in areas populated by poor and Indigenous women. In 1997, 110,000 sterilizations were performed. They often took place without informed consent or high medical quality. Several women died from botched operations.[12] Between 1995 and 2000 in Peru, over 200,000 Indigenous women and 22,000 Indigenous men were sterilized.[13] USAID itself emphasized family planning over coercive measures. But it did endorse the near-impossible fertility targets that allowed these abuses to occur.

Such stories are not uncommon. Until the 1990s, mainstream agencies like the UN Population Fund often rejected voluntary methods of contraception and family planning for population control. This changed somewhat in 1994, at the International Conference on Population and Development in Cairo. After years of protest of involuntary and coerced sterilization by women of colour and women from the Global South, the conference began to integrate ideas of reproductive rights and women's right to choose into population programs. Now, the story goes like this. Empower women with a full range of reproductive options, and a reduction in population will naturally follow.

In many ways, the focus on empowerment represents a success. However, some advocates remain suspicious about population initiatives. They believe the feminist agenda has been co-opted. Population control, not advancing women's rights, is the central goal of these initiatives. Population control programs most often target the Global South or marginalized communities in the North. Rarely do we hear that the population of wealthy elites need to be controlled. Sterilization abuses like those seen in Peru and India continue, sometimes with the support of international agencies. Since population initiatives are often integrated into neoliberal agendas, they can be seen as contributing to poverty and powerlessness. People who live in conditions of poverty and powerlessness have a minimal range of choices. They don't have a meaningful right to choose.

The Rand Corporation, a U.S.-based think tank, offers research advice to the U.S. army. Its Population Matters program studies population policy issues. This bizarre organization has been a subject of suspicion and mockery. (Its 1968 report *UFOs: What to Do?* is said to have inspired *Star Trek*.) But it receives government funding and appears to influence U.S. government policy.

In 2000, a worldwide anti-globalization movement challenging free market capitalism was at its height. The Rand Corporation published *The Security Dynamics of Demographic Factors,* a document warning of the danger of population growth in a time of resistance. "Some high-fertility developing states contain radical political movements on the fringes of their political spectra," it said. With burgeoning young populations, the document warned of the possibility of "full scale revolution."[14] In the wake of the 9/11 terror attacks in 2001, the Rand Corporation published *Regional Demographics and the War on Terrorism*. This report suggested that high fertility rates "contribute to extremism in Muslim regions," since "disenchantment and hopelessness can make large numbers of youths more susceptible to recruitment by movements like Al Qu'aida."[15]

Such statements make it plain that population control programs often have political interests at their heart. No wonder so many of these initiatives end in the tragic abuse of women's bodies. Advocates may believe in providing reproductive options to women. But women's choices are sacrificed for a larger political goal.

Population control is also experiencing a bit of a resurgence among some environmentalists. They blame overpopulation for a number of ills, including climate change.[16] Population Matters, a U.K.-based charity, argues for population control as a way to reduce carbon emissions. Family planning, it claims, is cheaper than low-carbon technologies.[17] The organization is supported by some big names: primatologist Jane Goodall, media broadcaster David Attenborough, and Paul Ehrlich, author of *The Population Bomb*. It recently introduced the website PopOffsets (www.popoffsets.com). Through this site, people can offset their carbon footprint by donating to family planning initiatives.

Population Matters and organizations like it advocate for voluntary means of contraception and family planning. But they are wading into dangerous territory. By making people's bodies part of the battle to prevent environmental catastrophe, they are putting reproductive rights at risk. We can learn from history how power dynamics are likely to play out. These policies and ideas will surely target those who are already the most marginalized. The reproductive autonomy of poor people will be seen as expendable. It will be sacrificed for the supposed greater good of environmental protection.

Such ideas also distract from the bigger threats facing our global environment. An economic system, for example, that encourages

Reproductive Justice Is Environmental Justice

Some environmentalists would have us believe that to avoid environmental disaster, it is necessary to limit the population—at any cost to people's reproductive or bodily autonomy. But struggles for reproductive justice and environmental justice need not be in conflict. They may, in fact, be deeply intertwined.

The Native Youth Sexual Health Network works in Canada and the United States. This organization draws connections between environmental and reproductive justice. Showing that environmental mega-projects leave behind toxic contaminants with reproductive health impacts, it says environmental violence must be addressed as a reproductive justice issue. For example, in Indigenous communities near mining, drilling, or logging sites, the network cites evidence of increased breast milk contamination, disproportionate rates of cancer in reproductive organs, an increase in developmental delays and learning disabilities in children, and an increase in miscarriages and stillbirths. The network also notes that extractive industries place stress on nearby communities. This leads to an increase in social problems.

The network sees an intrinsic connection between the damage done to the land and environment and damage done to the bodies of women and children. As a result, it resists projects like the Alberta tar sands oil development and pipelines that would allow for its expansion. It takes this stand as part of its sexual and reproductive justice agenda.

Source: Native Youth Sexual Health Network, "NYSHN Statement to the National Energy Board Regarding Line 9 Pipeline Proposal," www.nativeyouthsexualhealth.com, Oct. 18, 2013.

unsustainable economic growth and resource consumption. It is telling that those who argue for population control do not suggest it is necessary in the Global North. Resource consumption in the North far outstrips that of countries of the South. Malthus used population growth to distract from the problems of the emerging capitalist system. It is used today to distract from the environmental consequences of economic growth and inequality. This is dangerous for reproductive justice.

LONG-ACTING CONTRACEPTIVES

Another battlefield for reproductive justice is that of long-acting, provider-controlled contraceptives. These drugs are also known as LARCs—long-acting reversible contraceptives. Norplant and Depo-Provera are common examples. Norplant (and Jadelle, a similar drug) provides effective contraception for up to five years. A doctor implants rods that release hormones into the body. Depo-Provera provides contraception for three months. A doctor administers a hormone injection.

Supporters claim that these drugs add an important contraceptive option. But the drugs have been wildly controversial. A litany of health risks is associated with their use. And like sterilization, they can been used to coercively control the population of vulnerable groups.

With long-acting methods, you do not need to remember (or choose) to take them, as you would the pill. The effects of injectable drugs are not easily reversed. And removing implanted drugs is a complex procedure that must be performed by health professionals, who are sometimes unwilling or unable to do it.[18]

Norplant underwent its first human trials in Brazil, Haiti, and Bangladesh. It was tested in ethically questionable conditions.[19] In Brazil the trials were stopped, in response to protests from women's health advocates. But despite widespread reports of severe side effects and abuse, the drug was approved. During the trials in Bangladesh, some women had difficulty getting the drug removed when they requested it.[20] The rationale for refusal was often that the drug was too expensive to be "wasted" by removal before five years. This is an affront to people's ability to control their own fertility. In other cases, it was difficult to find a doctor able to remove the device—or to deal with the side effects. This is not surprising. Structural Adjustment Policies have caused a general lack of health care services in the Global South. Norplant did not give women increased control over their bodies. It put their bodies under the control of health professionals and population control organizations.

As long-acting drugs gained acceptance, they began to be used in the Global North. Additional issues arose. One was side effects. For Norplant, they include headaches, depression, weight gain, nausea, ovarian cysts, irregular menstrual bleeding, nerve damage, and increased risk of stroke and heart attack. For Depo-Provera, they are nausea, depression, increased risk of osteoporosis, nervousness, irregular menstrual bleeding, decreased resistance to sexually transmitted infections, and increased risk of breast, uterine, and cervical cancers.[21] These can be serious effects. Over four hundred women in the United Kingdom filed a lawsuit against Norplant because of the severe side effects they developed. Norplant withdrew from the U.K. market in 1999. That same year, Norplant manufacturers paid out over US\$50 million to settle similar claims in the United States.[22]

Given side effects like these, it isn't surprising that Norplant and Depo-Provera are most often used with vulnerable people. In Israel, xenophobic sentiments run high against African immigrants. In 2013, the country admitted that Ethiopian immigrants had been threatened or intimidated into taking injections of Depo-Provera. The result was a 50 percent decline in the birth rate in Israel's Ethiopian community.[23] In the United States, studies have shown that Depo-Provera is disproportionately used among Indigenous and African American women. Norplant has also been disproportionately given to African American women.[24]

Some women in the United States have reported being coerced into using long-acting contraceptives immediately after giving birth or having an abortion.[25] In several U.S. states, women convicted of child abuse or drug abuse have been offered the option of Norplant as an alternative to jail time. And in the 1990s, several states tried to enact legislation that would make Norplant use mandatory for these groups or require it for people to receive social assistance benefits.[26] In many states, Medicaid—the health insurance program for low-income individuals—covers the insertion of Norplant. But it does not cover the cost of removal.[27] The choice to use the drug is covered, in other words, but the choice to stop using it is not.

After Norplant was approved by the U.S. Food and Drug Administration in 1990, an article appeared in the *Philadelphia Inquirer* titled "Poverty and Norplant: Can Contraception Reduce the Underclass?"[28] It suggested that the drug be promoted as a solution to inner city poverty: "What if welfare mothers were offered an increased benefit for agreeing to use this new, safe, long-term contraceptive?" The article echoed a common sentiment. Because the impact of Norplant is temporary, its use for population control has been seen as less ethically problematic than permanent sterilization.

But permanent or not, Norplant and Depo-Provera are easily manipulated for political goals at the expense of people's control over their own reproduction. These drugs are often offered to those considered "not responsible" enough to take the pill. There is evidence that Depo-Provera was used as birth control on women in Canada before it was approved for that purpose. It was routinely given to institutionalized disabled women for "hygienic" reasons—that is, to prevent them from having a period.[29] Stereotypes that cast them as childlike or helpless make disabled women particularly vulnerable to being prescribed these sorts of medications. Since the drugs are long acting, this has potentially eugenic consequences.

In the United States, campaigns have aggressively promoted Norplant to teenagers, particularly in black communities. It is seen as a way to "solve" the issue of teen pregnancy. But while Norplant offers effective contraception, it doesn't address the real issues. High teen pregnancy rates are a result of factors including systemic poverty and high rates of sexual abuse.[30]

The use of long-acting contraceptives also raises a host of questions. Are contraceptive methods that rely so heavily on doctors appropriate? Do they take control out of the hands of the people who are using them? Feminist health advocates argue that the provider-controlled nature of Norplant and Depo-Provera tips an already unequal power relationship between women and health care providers. It makes it harder for people to become better-educated advocates for their own health and bodies.[31] If someone knows the full range of available contraception options and is fully informed of the potential side effects, they could decide that Norplant or Depo-Provera was their best option. But in a world where reproductive options and bodies are heavily politicized, this kind of free choice is rarely a reality.

Today, newer forms of the IUD (intrauterine device) are being promoted as a safe and effective long-acting contraceptive. But the results from a 2010 study give us reason to be cautious. When health care providers were shown videos of hypothetical patients with different socio-economic characteristics, they were more likely to recommend IUDs to women of colour than to white women in the low-income bracket.[32] Meanwhile, anecdotally at least, young white women, especially if they don't have children, may be met with reluctance if they try to get an IUD. To make it easier to access, some reproductive health advocates are pushing for more widespread acceptance of this contraceptive method. But in advocating for IUDs, it is vitally important that they are not involuntarily pushed on those in more vulnerable situations. As far as we know, IUDs haven't been disproportionately prescribed to people of colour and low-income people. But we'd do well to keep in mind the ways these dynamics have played out in the not-so-distant past.[33]

LEARNING FROM HISTORY

We have not covered all the examples of coercive sterilization that continue today. In Australia, for example, reports have surfaced of intellectually disabled people being sterilized without consent.[34] Societal prejudices and systemic discrimination lead some people to be more strongly encouraged to undergo sterilization than others. In most places the requirement for consent to sterilization is more rigorous than in the past. But formal consent does not always mean that a person has freely chosen the procedure. For example, four Indigenous women in Canada approached the media in 2015. They told of being coerced into being sterilized by hospital staff shortly after giving birth.[35] Consent forms were signed. But the women were strongly encouraged by their doctors to undergo the procedure. And having just given birth, they were in a particularly vulnerable situation. I can only speculate about the prejudices at play. It sounds unlikely, though, that sterilization was brought up in the context of conversations around contraception that the women initiated.

The struggles against eugenics ideas and sterilization laws resulted in real gains for many people. But people continue to be prevented from becoming parents, often closer to home than we'd imagine. People are still targeted for sterilization because of their race, their disabilities, how much money they make, or where they live. I'd like to think we can do better—and avoid replicating the injustices of the past. Reproductive issues are intertwined with other social justice issues. They need to be addressed hand in hand.

6

TAKING ACTION

TOWARD
REPRODUCTIVE
JUSTICE

S OME of these stories are more than a little bit depressing. Botched abortions, unjust laws, forced sterilizations ... Some days it's hard not to feel overwhelmed in the face of such coordinated assaults on people's bodies and lives.

When that happens, I remind myself to take a closer look at these stories. For every injustice, you can also find inspiring examples of resistance. Students standing up to anti-abortion curricula. Women of colour advocating for more inclusive visions of justice. Lawyers standing up to fight oppressive laws. There are doctors and midwives fighting hospital bureaucracy. Women and trans people standing up to doctors. Nuns fighting churches. Health care collectives, childcare collectives, and other ways people organize to support each other. There are people making art, writing articles, holding protests, opening clinics, and starting organizations.

Most examples of resistance will never make the news. Sometimes we hear about activism if it leads to a policy change. But rarely are we shown the hundreds of smaller acts that paved the way for that change to occur. This can make fighting for change seem impossible. Or it may feel that with limited resources, you can't do anything useful. But if experience has taught me anything, it is that the biggest myth of all is that power can't shift and that things can't change. Even if that change is slower and more unpredictable than we might like.

TOWARD A VISION OF JUSTICE

In this book, I've focused on abortion and coercive sterilization. But many more issues determine who can control their own reproduction. Access to sex ed, birth control, and in vitro fertilization. Midwifery care, paid maternity leave, and childcare. These issues are just as important. They, too, determine how much control you have over whether or not to have a child. There are also cultural issues. Gender stereotypes suggesting that the natural role of women is as mothers, or casting people of any gender as weak if they devote themselves to parenting. Ideas about who is and isn't fit to parent. The sexual objectification of women and girls.

There's the fight against sexual violence. In the United Kingdom, one-quarter of women will experience domestic violence, and 30 percent of this violence will start during pregnancy.[1] In fact, pregnancy is generally recognized as a risk factor for increased sexual violence. There's the fight for economic equity. People need adequate resources to have and to raise children, or to pay for contraception and abortion. There's the movement to end exploitative relationships between the Global North and the Global South. And to end so many states' colonial policies toward Indigenous peoples. We need to fight against population control in all its forms.

And the list doesn't end here. The tricky thing about working on reproductive issues is that it's not about one issue. To support the decisions and autonomy of individuals, families, and communities, we need to work for justice on all levels—economic, gender, sexual, racial, disability, environmental.

As women and trans people of colour push us to look beyond reproductive rights toward reproductive justice, the list of issues keeps expanding. We cannot limit ourselves to working on single issues. Patriarchy, colonialism, racism, and economic injustice interact in our lives and in our communities. This can, I admit, make the issues seem impossibly big. But it also means that all around us, people are fighting for reproductive justice.

Take, for example, an issue of utmost importance where I live, in Canada. An alarming number of Indigenous women have gone missing or been murdered. Between 1980 and 2014, Royal Canadian Mounted Police statistics show that 1,017 Indigenous women were murdered, and another 164 went missing.[2] Amnesty International has called the situation "nothing less than a national human rights crisis."[3] This issue has been a focus of the Native Youth Sexual Health Network. It has partnered with No More Silence and Families of Sisters in Spirit to launch a community database documenting the violence (www.itstartswithus-mmiw.com). Against the backdrop of Canada's history of wanting to rid the land of Indigenous peoples, we can understand these deaths and disappearances as a reproductive issue. The government may not be directly responsible for the deaths. But its colonial policies have created the conditions for them to occur. The conditions of poverty, racism, and violence against women make Indigenous women particularly vulnerable to violence. And according to the Native Women's Association of Canada, 88 percent of missing and murdered Indigenous women are mothers.[4] Women are often responsible for childbearing and raising children. Their disappearance from the lives of their children and communities has a drastic impact on the future of Indigenous people in this country. Like residential schools, this phenomenon is likely to have an intergenerational impact. Among cases for which information is available, over 440 Indigenous children have suffered the trauma of losing their mothers.

In the United States and Canada, the last few years have seen massive mobilizations in response to the violence faced by black people, particularly from police. Operating under the banner Black Lives Matter, the movement coalesced when a police officer responsible for the 2012 shooting of black teenager Trayvon Martin in Sanford, Florida, was acquitted. It demands an end to racist injustices that leave white people who kill free and innocent black people dead. Trust Black Women works to counter campaigns to limit black women's access to abortion, and affirms the ability of black women to make their own family planning decisions. This organization explains that both Black Lives Matter and reproductive justice are "movements to affirm the value of Black lives, to protect the dignity and autonomy of Black bodies, and to dismantle the systems that harm and oppress Black communities."[5] The connection becomes clearer when we consider that black people who are killed by police or imprisoned are also someone's children. Sometimes they are parents themselves. Mothers of the Movement has highlighted this connection. This group of women, mothers of many of the prominent black people shot by police, made headlines in 2016 when they joined Beyoncé onstage at the Video Music Awards and appeared at the Democratic National Convention.

Black Lives Matter has also highlighted the injustice in our justice systems. Black communities are disproportionately criminalized and surveilled by police. In 2010, black women in the United States were incarcerated at three times the rate of white women. Similarly, in Canada, Indigenous people account for almost 25 percent of the imprisoned population, despite being only 4 percent of Canada's population as a whole. One-third of women in Canadian prisons are Indigenous. Black people account for almost 10 percent of Canada's prisoners, but less than 3 percent of the total population.[6]

These statistics show the racism in our prison systems. They give particular significance to the reproductive injustices that prisoners face. In many U.S. states, women in prison are shackled during labour and delivery. They are cruelly prevented from making the natural movements of childbirth. One in twenty-five women in the state prison system is pregnant when admitted to prison. Most children born to women in prison are immediately separated from their mothers. Of women in state prisons, 62 percent have children who are minors.[7] Although prisoners are legally allowed to access abortions, in many facilities they are prevented from doing so.[8] So women in prison and their families face some serious barriers to self-determining their reproductive lives.

Reproductive justice organizations are addressing these issues. Forward Together has collaborated on community-based research on the social, emotional, and financial impact that having loved ones in prison has on families and communities. The Prison Birth Project, based in Massachusetts, provides doula care, childbirth classes, and other supports for women and trans people in prison. It played a role in getting an anti-shackling law passed in the state in 2014. It has since worked to ensure that local prisons comply with the law. The Birthing Behind Bars project of WORTH—an organization of formerly and currently incarcerated women—likewise helped to pass an anti-shackling law in New York State.

Justice issues might seem disparate—like the fights for decolonization, racial justice, and prison justice. But you can see that they are concretely related to the fight for reproductive justice. Sometimes the media will slam activists for not knowing what they want, or for having a laundry list of unfocused issues. But these issues can't be addressed in a vacuum. Doing so risks focusing on the issues that are most relevant to privileged communities. This happened in the historical feminist and reproductive rights movements. The feminist movement sometimes replicated the very power dynamics that it sought to dismantle. As we move forward, those of us working on reproductive issues need to be supporters and allies of all of these diverse movements. That way we can avoid the mistakes of the past.

TAKING ACTION

Reproductive issues are personal and intimate. I believe in starting with the issues that are closest to me and my communities. This means we become advocates for ourselves and those close to us. It means ensuring we have access to the services and support we need to be in control of our own bodies. With so many barriers to accessing reproductive services, this alone can be a significant form of everyday resistance. In a society with such inadequate sexual education, offering a friend advice on where to get information on birth control or an abortion can be almost radical.

When you want to think bigger, take a look around you to see where to start. We're generally most effective working with the people and issues we know best. Students might join or start a club that addresses reproductive and social justice issues at their school. If you are religious, you might start by seeking out people in your faith community with similar ideas. Artists might look to the ways other artists have engaged with these issues. For example, the New York–based Words of Choice theatre company presents a Reproductive Justice Walking Tour around Manhattan, with discussions and performances along the way. If you're skilled at writing, you might submit op-eds to your local media or publish your own zines or blogs. Organizing doesn't have to feel like a chore. Connect your activism to work you enjoy, and make it fun. In response to an anti-abortion law in the state, people in Michigan staged a HANDS OFF! flash mob in protest. (Lyrics: "It's my vagina, so hands off crazy!" to the tune of Carly Rae Jepsen's "Call Me Maybe.")

Starting with ourselves doesn't mean not caring about the barriers to reproductive justice that other people face. Far from it. Those of us who have more privilege in society also need to look at where we hold power in society, and the ways in which we are implicated in reproductive injustices. As Jessica Yee (now Danforth) has said, "Actualizing [reproductive justice] beyond a hot, new buzz word still has a long way to go and it has to start with being honest about where we are at and what's really going on in terms of racism, sexism, classism, white supremacy, homophobia, transphobia, ableism and more—not just systemically, but what we ourselves are complicit in as well."[9] This can be difficult work. But it is essential if we are going to avoid the mistakes of the past.

Starting with the issues most relevant to you *and* supporting a broader scope of reproductive justice issues may sound contradictory. But it needn't be. The reproductive justice movement allows us to think about issues in a broader context, even if we are working on a specific one. In other words, let's say abortion access is the issue you care most about. Try thinking about your work as just one small sliver in a movement for people to exercise control over all aspects of their own reproduction. And lend your support to people working on those other aspects when you can.

You can also look for ways to relate your own situation to the bigger picture. A great example is the support reproductive justice organizations have been giving to the Fight for $15. This campaign, led by workers in the fast-food industry in the United States and Canada, advocates for raising the minimum wage to fifteen dollars an hour. Many workers consider that to be a living wage. The campaign got New York State and Seattle, Washington, to raise their local rates, and in April 2015, held what some suggest was the largest protest of low-wage workers in U.S. history.[10] Most of us work for minimum wage at some point in our lives. So this is a place where your personal situation likely intersects with a bigger campaign. In a political climate where access to abortion and other reproductive health services is limited both geographically and financially, low-wage workers face particular barriers. Especially where health and social services are being slashed. This was recognized by activists in St. Louis, Missouri, who marked International Women's Day in 2015 with a rally in support of the fifteen-dollars-an-hour minimum wage and to protest the terrible access to abortion in the state. There is only one abortion clinic in Missouri, and recent legislation has enforced one of the longest abortion waiting periods in the country.

When you consider the barriers to access to reproductive health care, increasing the minimum wage could be just as important as changing the abortion laws. Your ability to decide whether or not to have children will be limited by a lack of financial security. And more than 55 percent of those making minimum wage in the United States are women.[11] It quickly becomes clear why the Fight for $15 is an aspect of a fight for reproductive justice. And it's a part that many of us can relate to on a personal level.

Another great example was the response of some doctors and health care practitioners to 2012 cuts to refugee health care in Canada. These cuts threatened the ability of refugees to access reproductive and other health services. Doctors organized themselves to oppose the cuts. Others provided health care to refugees even in the absence of government funding. Solidarity with others is strongest when you're clear about who you are and where you come from. Then it springs from relationship, rather than just trying to help.

Your voice may, on its own, not make that much noise. But in a chorus of other voices, seemingly small actions can make a big difference. I recently received news that the hospital in the town I live in was threatening to close its women's clinic. This was the only facility in the area that provided abortions. Apparently the hospital received dozens of calls and emails about that decision expressing everything from concern to outrage. And this was before the news had been made public or reported in the media. These voices seem to have been effective. The public outrage changed the tone of discussions, and the clinic remained open. This will make a tangible difference to the hundreds of people who need to access the clinic's services every year. The bottom line? Collective action can work.

Taking action doesn't need to be fancy or involved. Talk to family members about some of the stereotypes you've learned to see beyond. Challenge a racist or sexist comment, or support a friend who's struggling with these issues. Small day-to-day changes add up. If they are done often enough by enough people over a long enough period of time, they can create lasting cultural change.

This is important to know. It is a myth that we can't change things. But the people in power don't want us to realize that. That is why reproductive issues are so often framed as issues of morality rather than politics. It distracts from the power imbalances at their heart, imbalances that are neither natural nor inevitable. Don't be fooled. Reproductive issues are political. And that means they can be changed.

If we work together, if we see the big picture, we can move beyond reproductive rights. We can achieve something that truly looks like reproductive justice.

Get involved!
Find out more at firedupbooks.ca.

NOTES

INTRODUCTION

1 "Forced Sterilization in Puerto Rico," Family Planning blog, www.stanford.edu, Oct. 23, 2008; "Puerto Rico," Eugenics Archive, http://eugenicsarchive.ca.

2 Dorothy Roberts, *Killing the Black Body: Race, Reproduction and the Meaning of Liberty* (New York: Pantheon, 1997).

3 Karen Stote, *An Act of Genocide: Colonialism and the Sterilization of Aboriginal Women* (Winnipeg: Fernwood, 2015).

4 Ruth Compton Brouwer, "Ironic Interventions: CUSO Volunteers in India's Family Planning Campaign, 1960s to 1970s," *Social History* 43, 86 (2010), 279–313.

5 Hence the term "reproductive justice," coined by women of colour to point to the convergence of power dynamics around class, gender, and race in reproductive issues. This term will be introduced in more depth in chapter 1.

6 Jessica Shaw, *Reality Check: A Close Look at Accessing Abortion Services in Canadian Hospitals* (Ottawa: Canadians for Choice, 2006).

7 Turkey: Shena Cavallo, "Access to Abortion in Turkey: No Laughing Matter," International Women's Health Coalition, http://iwhc.org, Feb. 17, 2015. Austria: "Europe's Abortion Rules," BBC News, www.bbc.com,

Feb. 12, 2007; "Austria Abortion Policies," United Nations Department of Economic and Social Affairs: Population Division, www.un.org.

8 Jonathan Watts, "El Salvador: Where Women Are Thrown into Jail for Losing a Baby," *Guardian*, www.theguardian.com, Dec. 17, 2015, "Can Chile's Abortion Rights Reforms Overcome Staunch Religious Opposition?," *Guardian*, Aug. 3, 2015.

9 World Health Organization (WHO), "Unsafe Abortion: The Preventable Pandemic," journal paper, Sexual and Reproductive Health 4, www.who.int.

10 See Loretta Ross, "Understanding Reproductive Justice: Transforming the Pro-Choice Movement," *Off Our Backs* 36,4 (2006), www.law.berkeley.edu, 14–19. We'll look at the term "reproductive justice" in more detail in chapter 1.

11 Martha L. Raimon, Kristen Weber, and Amelia Esenstad, "Better Outcomes for Older Youth of Color in Foster Care," American Bar Association, http://americanbar.org, March 25, 2015.

12 "A Guide to Australia's Stolen Generations," Creative Spirits: Teacher and Student Resources, www.creativespirits.info; Peter Read, *The Stolen Generation: The Removal of Aboriginal Children in New South Wales, 1883–1969* (New South Wales Department of Aboriginal Affairs, 2006).

13 Native American youth: "Time for Reform: A Matter of Justice for American Indian and Alaskan Native Children," National Indian Child Welfare Association, www.nicwa.org, 2007. Australia: Steering Committee for the Review of Government Service Provision, *Report on Government Services 2015: Indigenous Compendium*, Productivity Commission, Canberra, www.pc.gov.au. Canada: Cindy Blackstock, "Reconciliation Means Not Saying Sorry Twice: Lessons from Child Welfare in Canada," in *Speaking My Truth: Reflections on Reconciliation and Residential School*, ed. Shelagh Rogers, Mike Degagné, Jonathan Dewar, and Glen Lowry (Aboriginal Healing Foundation, 2013), 163–75.

14 Pamela Palmater, "Unstated Paternity Still Excluding Indigenous Women from 'Indian' Status," rabble.ca Blogs, Oct. 21, 2014.

15 Laura Erickson-Schroth, ed., *Trans Bodies, Trans Selves: A Resource for the Transgender Community* (New York: Oxford University Press, 2014).

CHAPTER 1. DEFINING REPRODUCTIVE ISSUES

1 This discussion draws heavily on Asian Communities for Reproductive Justice [Forward Together], "A New Vision," 2005, www.forwardtogether.org.

2 United Nations, *The Road to Dignity by 2030: Ending Poverty, Transforming All Lives and Protecting the Planet,* Synthesis Report of the Secretary-General on the Post-2015 Agenda, www.un.org, Dec. 4, 2014.

3 Loretta Ross, "Understanding Reproductive Justice" (SisterSong Reproductive Health Collective, 2006). This article is drawn on throughout this section on reproductive justice. A 2011 update is online at www.trustblackwomen.org.

4 Ross, "Understanding Reproductive Justice: Transforming the Pro-Choice Movement," *Off Our Backs* 36,4 (2006), 15.

5 Angela Davis, *Women, Race and Class* (New York: Random House, 1982), 354–55.

6 Loretta Ross, "Understanding Reproductive Justice" (SisterSong, 2006, updated 2011), Trust Black Women, www.trustblackwomen.org.

CHAPTER 2. MAKING ABORTION LEGAL

1 Pew Research Center, www.pewresearch.org/data.

2 Mark Kennedy, "New Poll Shows Most Canadians Support Abortion—with Some Restrictions," *National Post,* www.nationalpost.com, July 4, 2012.

3 "Sexual and Reproductive Health: Preventing Unsafe Abortion," World Health Organization, www.who.int.

4 WHO, "Unsafe Abortion: The Preventable Pandemic."

5 World Health Organization, *Unsafe Abortion: Global and Regional Estimates of the Incidence of Unsafe Abortion and Associated Mortality in 2008,* 6th ed. (2011).

6 "Abortion Laws Worldwide," Women on Waves, www.womenonwaves.org.

7 Boston Women's Health Book Collective, *Our Bodies, Ourselves* (New York: Touchstone, 2011), 337.

8   Barbara Ehrenreich and Deirdre English, *Witches, Midwives and Nurses: A History of Women Healers,* 2nd ed. (New York: Feminist Press, 2010).

9   Boston Women's Health Book Collective, *Our Bodies, Ourselves.*

10 Nicola Beisel and Tamara Kay, "Abortion, Race and Gender in Nineteenth Century America," *American Sociological Review* 69 (Aug. 2004), 498–518.

11 Ardath Whynacht, "The Road to Health Is Paved with 'Good Intentions': A Cautionary Three Part Tale for Global Health in the Spirit of Reproductive Justice," MA Thesis, Dalhousie University, 2010, https://dalspace.library.dal.ca.

12 Myra Feree, Gurhards Marx, Gamson Jurgen, William Anthony, and Dieter Rucht, *Shaping Abortion Discourse: Democracy and the Public Sphere in Germany and the United States* (Cambridge: Cambridge University Press, 2002).

13 U.S.: "The Impact of Illegal Abortion," Our Bodies Ourselves, www.ourbodiesourselves.org, March 23, 2014. U.K.: C.B. Goodhart, "The Frequency of Illegal Abortion," *Eugenics Review* 55,4 (1964). Canada: Vicki Saporta, "Introduction," 20th Anniversary of *Regina vs. Morgentaler*: Of What Difference: Reflections on the Judgement and Abortion in Canada Today, symposium cohosted by National Abortion Federation and Faculty of Law, University of Toronto, 2008, www.prochoice.org.

14 Childbirth by Choice Trust, *No Choice: Canadian Women Tell Their Stories of Illegal Abortion* (Toronto: Childbirth by Choice Trust, 1998).

15 Fran Moreland Johns, *Perilous Times: An Inside Look at Abortion before—and after—Roe v. Wade* (New York: YBK, 2013).

16 Canada: Pamela Cross, "Abortion in Canada: Legal but Not Accessible," YWCA Canada Discussion Paper, www.ywcatoronto.org, n.d. U.K.: Anna Browning, "The World of Vera Drake," BBC News, www.bbc.com, Feb. 23, 2005. U.S.: Boston Women's Health Book Collective, *Our Bodies, Ourselves,* "Abortion" chapter excerpted at www.feminist.com.

17 Johns, *Perilous Times.*

18 Connie Bryson, "I Had an Illegal Abortion in 1953: We Need *Roe v Wade* to Ensure No One Else Has To," *Guardian,* opinion, www.theguardian.com, Oct. 16, 2015.

19 Patricia G. Miller, "The Worst of Times: When Abortion Was Illegal and Desperation Reigned," *Psychology Today* (May/June 1993), 48–52.

20 U.S.: "The Impact of Illegal Abortion," Our Bodies Ourselves. U.K.: Diane Munday, Colin Francome, and Wendy Savage, "Twenty One Years of Legal Abortion," *British Medical Journal* 298,6682 (1989), 1231–34. Canada: Mary Ormsby, "The 'Abortion Caravan' Succeeded: Or Did It?," thestar.com, May 30, 2010.

21 W.D. Thomas, "The Badgley Report on the Abortion Law," *Canadian Medical Association Journal* 116,9 (1977), 966.

22 Dagmar Herzog, *Sexuality in Europe: A Twentieth Century History* (Cambridge: Cambridge University Press, 2011), 23.

23 Beth Palmer, "Lonely, Tragic, but Legally Necessary Pilgrimages: Transnational Abortion Travel in the 1970s," *Canadian Historical Review* 92,4 (2011), 637–64.

24 Ian Mylchreest, "'Sound Law and Undoubtedly Good Policy': *Roe v. Wade* in Historical Perspective," in *Politics of Abortion and Birth Control in Historical Perspective*, ed. Donald Critchlow (Penn State Press, 2010), 53–71.

25 Boston Women's Health Book Collective, *Our Bodies, Ourselves*, 787.

26 Willard Cates Jr., David A. Grimes, and Kenneth F. Schulz, "The Public Health Impacts of Legal Abortion: 30 Years Later," *Perspectives on Sexual and Reproductive Health* 35,1 (2004), 25–28, citing research from Cates et al., "Legalized Abortion: Effect on National Trends of Maternal and Abortion-Related Mortality (1940–1976)," *American Journal of Obstetrics and Gynecology* 132,2 (1978), 221–24.

27 Ibid.; "Reproductive Health Module: Section IV: Abortion," Harriet and Robert Heilbrunn Department of Population and Family Health, Columbia University Mailman School of Public Health, www.columbia.edu.

28 Boston Women's Health Book Collective, *Our Bodies, Ourselves*, 787.

29 Mexico: Allyn Gaestel and Allison Shelley, "Mexican Women Pay High Price for Country's Rigid Abortion Laws," *Guardian*, www.theguardian.com, Oct. 1, 2014. Ireland: here2help, www.here2help.ie; "How Much Does an Unplanned Pregnancy Actually Cost in Ireland?," Her, www.her.ie. Poland: Gabriela Baczynska, "More Polish Women Seen Seeking Abortions Abroad," Reuters, www.reuters.com, Aug. 26, 2010.

30 Henry McDonald, "Savita Halappanavar Died Due to Medical Misadventure, Inquest Finds," *Guardian*, www.theguardian.com, April 19, 2013; Jodi Jacobson, "Inquest Confirms Savita Halappanavar's Life Was Subordinated to Non-viable Fetus," *Rewire*, https://rewire.news, April 12, 2013.

31 "Chile Abortion Policies," United Nations Department of Economic and Social Affairs: Population Division, www.un.org.

32 Chile: "Chile: Abortion Law," Women on Waves, www.womenonwaves.org. Mexico: Allyn Gaestel and Allison Shelley, "Mexican Women Pay High Price for Country's Rigid Abortion Laws," *Guardian*, www.theguardian.com, Oct. 1, 2014. Ireland: Henry McDonald, "Abortion Activist: 'I'll Still Help Northern Irish Women Buy Pills,'" *Guardian*, April 5, 2016.

33 S. Arie, "Woman Dies after Doctors Fail to Intervene because of New Abortion Law in Nicaragua," *British Medical Journal* 333, 7577 (2006), 1037; Amnesty International, *The Total Abortion Ban in Nicaragua: Women's Lives and Health Endangered, Medical Professionals Criminalized*, AMR 43/001/2009 (London: Amnesty International Publications, 2009).

34 Mauritius: Ministry of Health and Quality of Life, Republic of Mauritius, "The National Sexual & Reproductive Health Policy," 2007. Zambia: W. Koster-Oyekan, "Why Resort to Illegal Abortion in Zambia? Findings of a Community-Based Study in Western Province," *Social Science and Medicine* 46, 10 (1998), 1303–12; Guttmacher Institute, "In Brief: Unsafe Abortion in Zambia," 2009 Series, No. 3, www.guttmacher.org. Turkey: F.A. Igde, R. Gué, M. Igde, and M. Yalcin, "Abortion in Turkey: Women in Rural Areas and the Law," *British Journal of General Practice* 58, 550 (2008), 370–73.

35 National Advocates for Pregnant Women, "Lesson from the U.S. Experience with Unborn Victims of Violence Laws," Abortion Rights Coalition of Canada, www.arcc-cdac.ca, n.d.

36 Fran Amery, "Intersectionality as Disarticulatory Practice: Sex-Selective Abortion and Reproductive Politics in the United Kingdom," *New Political Science* 37, 4 (2015), 509–24.

37 Rajani Bhatia, "Constructing Gender from the Inside Out: Sex-Selection Practices in the United States," *Feminist Studies* 36, 2 (2010), 260–91.

38 Amery, "Intersectionality as Disarticulatory Practice"; Jessica Shaw, "Abortion in Canada as a Social Justice Issue in Contemporary Canada," *Critical Social Work* 14,2 (2013).

39 Potdara Pritam, Baruab Alka, Dalviec Suchitra, and Paward Anand, "'If a Woman Has Even One Daughter, I Refuse to Perform the Abortion': Sex Determination and Safe Abortion in India," *Reproductive Health Matters* 23,45 (2015), 114–25.

40 "Turkey Drops Anti-abortion Legislation," *Al Jazeera*, www.aljazeera.com, June 22, 2012.

41 Constanze Letsch, "Istanbul Hospitals Refuse Abortions as Government's Attitude Hardens," *Guardian*, www.theguardian.com, Feb. 4, 2015.

42 This motion was tabled in the Canadian House of Commons by NDP MP Niki Ashton on May 8, 2014.

CHAPTER 3. MAKING ABORTION ACCESSIBLE

1   Shaw, *Reality Check*.

2   Ibid.

3   Tunisia: Fanny Ohier, "Abortion in Tunisia: A Shifting Landscape," tunisialive, www.tunisia-live.net, July 27, 2014. U.S.: "Unequal Access to Abortion," National Abortion Federation, https://prochoice.org.

4   Molly Redden, "It's Not Just Texas: Abortion Clinics Are Rapidly Closing in Liberal States, Too," *Guardian*, www.theguardian.com, Nov. 12, 2015.

5   Molly Redden, "Women in Texas May Have to Wait an Extra 20 Days for an Abortion," *Mother Jones*, www.motherjones.com, Oct. 5, 2015.

6   Manny Fernandez, "Abortion Restrictions Become Law in Texas, but Opponents Will Press Fight," *New York Times*, www.nytimes.com, July 18, 2013.

7   Redden, "Women in Texas."

8   U.S. Commission on Civil Rights, *Broken Promises: Evaluating the Native American Health Care System,* September 2004; *Access to Health Services for Remote First Nations Communities*, Reports of the Auditor General of Canada, Report 4, spring 2015, FA1-2015/1-4E-PDF, www.oag-bvg.gc.ca.

9   Jael Silliman, Marlene Gerber Fried, Loretta Ross, and Elena R.
    Gutiérrez, *Undivided Rights: Women of Color Organize for Reproductive
    Justice* (Cambridge, MA: South End Press, 2004), 111–18.

10 Guttmacher Institute, "In Brief: Facts on Abortion in Asia,"
    www.guttmacher.org, Nov. 2015.

11 Silliman, Fried, Ross, Gutiérrez, *Undivided Rights,* 113.

12 "In-Clinic Abortion Procedures," Planned Parenthood,
    www.plannedparenthood.org.

13 "Bans on Insurance Coverage of Abortion," American Civil Liberties
    Union, www.aclu.org.

14 Nancy Berlinger, "Conscience Clauses, Health Care Providers, and
    Parents," in *From Birth to Death and Bench to Clinic: The Hastings
    Center Bioethics Briefing Book for Journalists, Policymakers, and
    Campaigns,* ed. Mary Crowley (Garrison, NY: The Hastings Center,
    2008), 35–40, excerpted at www.thehastingscenter.org.

15 Medical Students for Choice, "Facts on Abortion," fact sheet,
    www.msfc.org, n.d.

16 Maya Dusenbery, "Undercover Audio of Texas Anti-choice Training
    Session Shows How the Movement Relies on Intimidation and Harass-
    ment," Feministing, www.feministing.com.

17 "Violence Statistics and History," National Abortion Federation,
    https://prochoice.org.

18 "Anti-choice Violence and Intimidation," fact sheet, NARAL Pro-
    Choice America, www.prochoiceamerica.org, n.d.

19 Robert P. Jones and Daniel Cox, *Chosen for What? Jewish Values in
    2012: Finding from the 2012 Jewish Values Survey* (Washington, DC:
    Public Religion Research Institute, 2012), www.prri.org.

20 K. Shapiro Gilla, "Abortion Law in Muslim Majority Countries: An
    Overview of Islamic Discourse with Policy Implications," *Health Policy
    and Planning* 29,4 (2014), 483–94, http://heapol.oxfordjournals.org.

21 Loretta Ross, "Re-enslaving Black Women," *On the Issues* online
    magazine, www.trustblackwomen.org, Fall 2008.

22 Roberts, *Killing the Black Body,* 56–104, 6 (quoted).

23 Davis, *Women, Race and Class,* 354–55.

24 U.S.: "'Crisis Pregnancy Centers' (CPCs)," NARAL Pro-Choice Amer-
    ica, www.prochoiceamerica.org. Canada: Joanna Smith, "Deception

Used in Counselling Women against Abortion," thestar.com, Aug. 7, 2010.

25 Smith, "Deception Used in Counselling Women against Abortion."

26 Tara Culp-Ressler, "Large Study Confirms That Abortion Is Extremely Safe," ThinkProgress, https://thinkprogress.org, Dec. 9, 2014.

27 NARAL Pro-Choice America, *Crisis Pregnancy Centers Lie: The Insidious Threat to Reproductive Freedom*, www.prochoiceamerica.org, [2015].

28 University of Guelph, York University, Memorial University, and Carleton University, among others.

29 "Morgentaler Clinic in Fredericton Performs Last Abortions before Closure," CBC News, www.cbc.ca, July 18, 2014.

30 Samantha Edwards and WLBZ, WCSH, "New Brunswick Women Coming to Maine for Abortions," WCSH6 Portland, www.wcsh6.com.

CHAPTER 4. THE HISTORY OF COERCIVE STERILIZATION

1 Daniel J. Kevles, "Eugenics and the Human Genome Project: Is the Past Prologue?," in *Justice and the Human Genome Project*, ed. Timothy F. Murphy, and Marc A. Lappe (Berkeley: University of California Press, 1994), 18.

2 Corey G. Johnson, "Female Inmates Sterilized in California Prisons without Approval," Reveal: From The Center for Investigative Reporting, www.revealnews.org, July 7, 2013.

3 Edwin Black, "Eugenics and the Nazis: The California Connection," *San Francisco Chronicle*, www.sfgate.com, Nov. 9, 2003.

4 Lutz Kaelber, "Eugenics: Compulsory Sterilization in 50 American States," presentation at 2012 Social Science History Association, available on University of Vermont website, www.uvm.edu.

5 Black, "Eugenics and the Nazis."

6 Stote, *An Act of Genocide*.

7 Denmark, Norway, Sweden: see individual country profiles at Eugenics Archive, http://eugenicsarchive.ca.

8 James A. Miller, "The Knife in the Closet: European Nations Begin to Confront Their Eugenic Pasts," Population Research Institute, www.pop.org, Nov. 1, 1997.

9   Ibid.

10 "Sweden," Eugenics Archive, http://eugenicsarchive.ca.

11 Glynis Whiting, *The Sterilization of Leilani Muir,* National Film Board of Canada, 1966, 46:59.

12 Kathryn Krase, "History of Forced Sterilization and Current U.S. Abuses," Our Bodies Ourselves, www.ourbodiesourselves.org, Oct. 1, 2014.

13 "Report Reveals That Romani Women Were Sterilised against Their Will in Sweden," Associated Press, European Roma Rights Centre, www.errc.org, Nov. 7, 1997.

14 *The Dark Unknown History: White Paper on Abuses and Rights Violations against Roma in the 20th Century*, Ministry of Culture, Sweden, Ds 2014:8, www.government.se.

15 James Savage, "University in Quest to Return Sami Bones," *Local,* www.thelocal.se, May 31, 2010.

16 Karen Stote, "The Coercive Sterilization of Aboriginal Women in Canada," *American Indian Culture and Research Journal* 36,3 (2012), 117–50.

17 "1976: Government Admits Forced Sterilization of Indian Women," Native Voices: Native Peoples' Concepts of Health and Illness, U.S. National Library of Medicine, www.nlm.nih.gov/nativevoices.

18 Stote, "The Coercive Sterilization of Aboriginal Women in Canada," 136–7.

19 David B. Hogan, "What's behind a Name: The Kaufman Prize of the Canadian Geriatrics Society," *Canadian Geriatrics Journal* 14,3 (2011).

20 "Sterilization Policy," Inclusion BC, www.inclusionbc.org.

21 Solveig C. Robinson, "Victoria Woodhull-Martin and *The Humanitarian* (1892–1901): Feminism and Eugenics at the Fin de Siècle," *Nineteenth-Century Gender Studies* 6,2 (summer 2010), www.ncgsjournal.com.

22 Michael M. Perry, "Was Victoria Woodhull the First Eugenicist?" introduction to Victoria Woodhull, *Lady Eugenicist: Feminist Eugenics in the Speeches and Writing of Victoria Woodhull* (San Francisco: Inkling Books, 2005).

23 Palash Ghosh, "Marie Stopes: Women's Rights Activist or Nazi Eugenicist?," *International Business Times*, www.ibtimes.com, Oct. 18, 2012.

24 Krase, "History of Forced Sterilization and Current U.S. Abuses."

25 "Forced Sterilization in Puerto Rico," Family Planning blog, www.stanford.edu, Oct. 23, 2008; "Puerto Rico," Eugenics Archive, http://eugenicsarchive.ca.

26 Andrea Smith, "Better Dead Than Pregnant: The Colonization of Native Women's Reproductive Health," in *Policing the National Body: Race, Gender and Criminalization*, ed. Jael Silliman and Anannya Bhattacharjee (Cambridge, MA: South End Press, 2002), 103–22.

CHAPTER 5. COERCIVE STERILIZATION TODAY

1 "24 Countries in Europe Require Sterilization of Trans People," Transgender Europe, http://tgeu.org, May 17, 2013.

2 For example, "My Transgender Sterilization, or Why My Consent Meant Nothing," Queer Anarchism, http://queeranarchism.tumblr.com.

3 OHCHR, UN Women, UNAIDS, UNDP, UNFPA, UNICEF, and WHO, *Eliminating Forced, Coercive and Otherwise Involuntary Sterilization: An Interagency Statement* (World Health Organization, 2014).

4 Jason Burke, "India Mass Sterilisation: Women Were 'Forced' into Camps, Say Relatives," *Guardian*, www.theguardian.com, Nov. 12, 2014.

5 Jason Burke, "Indian Women Die after State-Run Mass Sterilisation Campaign Goes Wrong," ibid.

6 Gethin Chamberlain, "UK Aid Helps to Fund Forced Sterilisation of India's Poor," *Guardian*, April 15, 2012.

7 Betsy Hartmann, "The Changing Faces of Population Control," *Policing the National Body*, ed. Silliman and Bhattacharjee, 269.

8 *Against Her Will: Forced and Coerced Sterilization of Women Worldwide*, Open Society Foundations, www.opensocietyfoundations.org, n.d.

9 "At the Hospital There Are No Human Rights: Reproductive and Sexual Rights Violations of Women Living with HIV in Namibia," Report by Namibian Women's Health Network, Northeastern University Law School, and International Human Rights Clinic at Harvard Law School, http://hrp.law.harvard.edu, n.d.

10 Zaynab Essack and Ann Strode, "'I Feel Like Half a Woman All the Time': The Impacts of Coerced and Forced Sterilisations on

HIV-Positive Women in South Africa," *Agenda: Empowering Women for Gender Equity* 26,2 (2012), 24–34.

11   *Against Her Will.*

12   Calvin Sims, "Using Gifts as Bait, Peru Sterilizes Poor Women," *New York Times,* Feb. 15, 1998, 1.

13   Amnesty International, "Peru: Over 2,000 Women in Peru Denied Justice," Peru: Right to Health campaign (AMR 46/003/2014), www.amnesty.org, Jan. 30, 2014.

14   Brian Nichiporuk, *The Security Dynamics of Demographic Factors* (Santa Monica, CA: RAND, 2000), www.rand.org.

15   Brian Nichiporuk, *Regional Demographics and the War on Terrorism* (Santa Monica, CA: RAND, 2003), www.rand.org, reprinted *from Royal United Services Institute for Defence Studies (RUSI) Journal* 148,1 (2003).

16   Haartman, "The Changing Faces of Population Control."

17   www.populationmatters.org

18   Roberts, *Killing the Black Body*, 127–33.

19   Deborah Cadbury, *The Human Laboratory,* documentary, 1995.

20   Karen Hardee, Sandor Balogh, and Michele T. Villinski, "Three Countries' Experience with Norplant Introduction," *Health Policy and Planning* 12,3 (1997), 199–213.

21   Committee on Women, Population, and the Environment (CWPE) at Adelphi University, "Dangerous Contraceptives: Norplant and Depo-Provera," http://temp-cwpe.gaiahost.net, July 27, 2006.

22   Ibid.

23   Talia Nesher, "Israel Admits Ethiopian Women Were Given Birth Control Shots," *Haaretz*, www.haaretz.com, Jan. 27, 2013.

24   Thomas W. Volscho, "Racism and Disparities in Women's Use of Depo-Provera Injection in the Contemporary USA," *Critical Sociology* 37,5 (2011), 673–88; Darcy Burrell, "The Norplant Solution: Norplant and the Control of African American Motherhood," *UCLA Women's Law Journal* 5,2 (1995), 401–44.

25   CWPE, "Dangerous Contraceptives."

26   "Norplant: A New Contraceptive with the Potential for Abuse," American Civil Liberties Union, www.aclu.org.

27 CWPE, "Dangerous Contraceptives."

28 Dec. 12, 1990.

29 DisAbled Women's Network, "DAWN Toronto Factsheet on Reproductive Rights," in *Canadian Women's Issues: Volume 1: Strong Voices*, ed. Ruth Roach Pierson, Marjorie Griffin Cohen, Paula Bourne, and Philinda Masters (Toronto, James Lorimer and Company, 1988).

30 Roberts, *Killing the Black Body*, 117–22.

31 CWPE, "Dangerous Contraceptives."

32 C. Dehlendorf, R. Ruskin, K. Grumbach, E. Vittinghoff, K. Bibbins-Domingo, D. Schillinger, and J. Steinauer, "Recommendations for Intrauterine Contraception: A Randomized Trial of the Effects of Patients' Race/Ethnicity and Socioeconomic Status," *American Journal of Obstetrics and Gynecology* 203,4 (2010).

33 Jenny A. Higgins, "Celebration Meets Caution: LARC's Boons, Potential Busts, and the Benefits of a Reproductive Justice Approach," *Contraception* 89 (2014), 237–41.

34 Bridie Jabour, "UN Examines Australia's Forced Sterilisation of Women with Disabilities," *Guardian*, www.theguardian.com, Nov. 10, 2015.

35 "Another Saskatoon Woman Says She Was Sterilized against Her Will," CBC News, www.cbc.ca, Dec. 16, 2015.

CHAPTER 6. TAKING ACTION

1 "Domestic Abuse," NHS Choices, www.nhs.uk.

2 Royal Canadian Mounted Police, "Missing and Murdered Aboriginal Women: A National Operational Review" (RCMP, 2014), www.rcmp-grc.gc.ca.

3 Amnesty International Canada, "No More Stolen Sisters," www.amnesty.ca.

4 Native Women's Association of Canada, "Fact Sheet: Missing and Murdered Aboriginal Women and Girls," http://nwac.ca, n.d.

5 "Trust Black Women Statement of Solidarity with Black Lives Matter," Trust Black Women, www.trustblackwomen.org.

6 U.S.: "Fact Sheet: Incarcerated Women and Girls," The Sentencing Project, www.sentencingproject.org, updated Nov. 2015. Canada:

Office of the Correctional Investigator, "The Changing Face of Canada's Prisons: Correctional Investigator Reports on Ethno-Cultural Diversity in Corrections," Government of Canada, www.oci-bec.gc.ca, Nov. 26, 2013.

7   "Fact Sheet: Incarcerated Women and Girls," The Sentencing Project.

8   Diana Kasdan, "Abortion Access for Incarcerated Women: Are Correctional Health Practices in Conflict with Constitutional Standards?," *Perspectives on Sexual and Reproductive Health* 41,1 (2009), 59–62.

9   Jessica Yee, "Reproductive Justice: For Me, for You, for Real, for Now," Native Youth Sexual Health Network, www.nativeyouthsexualhealth.com, 2010.

10 Steven Greenhouse and Jana Kasperkevic, "Fight for $15 Swells into Largest Protest by Low-Wage Workers in US History," *Guardian*, www.theguardian.com, April 15, 2015.

11 National Economic Council, Council of Economic Advisers, Domestic Policy Council, and Department of Labor, "The Impact of Raising the Minimum Wage on Women: And the Importance of Ensuring a Robust Tipped Minimum Wage," U.S. Government Report, www.whitehouse.gov, March 2014.

INDEX

United Nations Population Fund, 111–12

United States
    abortion access in, 9, 44, 64–66
    abortion law in, 24, 49–50, 54, 56
    anti-abortion violence in, 70–71
    eugenics policies in, 91–92
    health care system in, 67–68
    public opinion on abortion, 39
    sterilization in, 87, 90, 91–92, 93, 95, 97–98, 103, 104

university campuses, and anti-abortion initiatives, 74–75, 83

unsafe abortions, 10–11, 40
    experiences of, 44–47
    fatality rates, 46–47
    risks and complications, 40–41

USAID, 112

V

violence, anti-abortion, 70–71

W

Walia, Harsha, 89

white supremacy, 5
    and contraception, 14
    and state control over reproduction, 4, 5, 6–7
    and sterilization campaigns, 87–88, 91, 95–97

Women on Waves, 26

Woodhull, Victoria, 99–100

Y

Yee, Jessica, 126